# WORLD
# SOCIALIST
# REVOLUTION

# WORLD SOCIALIST REVOLUTION

GERALD MCISAAC

Printed in the United States of America
Parchment Global Publishing

1-888-266-0922
www.parchmentglobalpublishing.com
info@parchmentglobalpublishing.com

ISBN 978-1-959483-36-6 (sc)
ISBN 978-1-959483-37-3 (hc)
ISBN 978-1-959483-38-0 (e)

Library of Congress Control Number: 2023903127

History
2023.01.09

# CONTENTS

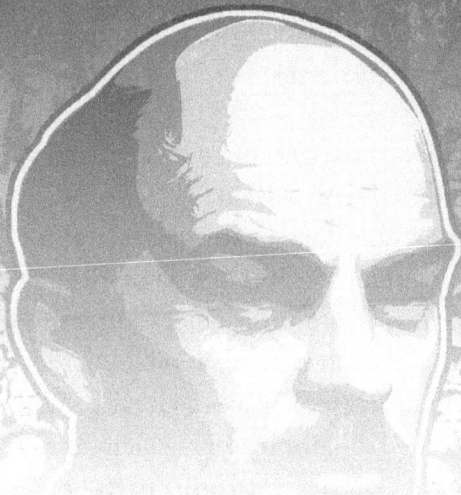

# CHAPTER 1

## The Industrial Revolution and the Creation of New Revolutionary Classes

Recently, it has been brought to my attention that over the years, numerous civilizations have come into existence. They all prospered, became ever more powerful, rose to a peak, and then fell into decline. In the western world, the Roman Empire is supremely well known. As the Roman Empire lasted for hundreds of years, people in those days were fond of saying that "Rome is Eternal".

Of course, nothing is "eternal", and the fate of the Roman Empire is well known. It went the "way of all empires", so to speak.

Yet that does not mean that our civilization must "follow suit", as so many "philosophers" maintain. There is a huge difference between our civilization and all previous civilizations. Our civilization is the one and only civilization to have experienced an industrial revolution!

Historians are agreed that the industrial revolution was the greatest thing to happen to humanity, since the domestication of plants and animals. In this, they are absolutely correct!

With that in mind, perhaps a little explanation is in order.

The industrial revolution first took place in Great Britain between the years of 1720 to 1760, for reasons which do not directly concern us. From there, it spread to other parts of the world, and in fact, it is still spreading.

At that time, in Britain, there existed a small, rather unimportant class of people, merchants who lived in town and referred to themselves as "burghers". They regarded the industrial revolution as an "opportunity", a chance to become supremely wealthy. It was merely a matter of investing their money in factories, mills, mines and other "means of production", as well as railroads, shipping lines and other "means of transportation". In that way, the "raw materials" can be taken to the "point of production", and the "finished product" can be "taken to market". They also invested in banks and other "financial institutions".

I believe those are the correct technical expressions of the capitalists.

As a result of this, the class of burghers became transformed into a class of capitalists. The name burgher became altered to that of "bourgeois". Those who became supremely rich became known as the "bourgeoisie".

Incidentally, some readers may find these technical terms to be tiresome, and perhaps they are. Yet it is important to become familiar with them, as otherwise, our class enemies will use our lack of knowledge against us.

For the purposes of this article, I am mainly concerned with the fact that the industrial revolution gave birth to two different classes, both revolutionary.

As Marx and Engels stated, quite clearly, in the Communist Manifesto:

"The history of all hitherto existing society is the history of class struggles.

"Freeman and slave, patrician and plebeian, lord and serf, guild master and journeyman, in a word, oppressor and oppressed, stood in constant opposition to one another, carried on an uninterrupted, now hidden, now open fight, a fight that each time ended, either of a revolutionary reconstitution of society at large, or of the common ruin of the contending classes.

"In the earlier epochs of history, we find almost everywhere a complicated arrangement of society into various orders, a manifold gradation of social rank. In ancient Rome, we have patricians, knights, plebeians, slaves; in the Middle Ages, feudal lords, vassals, guild masters, journeymen, apprentices, serfs; in almost all of these classes, again, subordinate gradations".

It is clear that in the case of the Roman Empire, for example, the "fight" of the "contending classes" ended in the "common ruin of the contending classes", as there was no "revolutionary reconstitution of society at large". In short, the Roman Empire rose to a peak, fell into decline, and eventually rotted away. This is characteristic of most civilization.

It is also clear that our civilization has also passed its peak, and is now in decline. Our roads, bridges, railways and transportation network, as well as our buildings, that which is usually referred to as the "super structure", is in desperate need of repair. Our books of science, which are taught in schools, are nothing less than a farce. The existence of classes, at least here in North America, is denied. Yet that does not mean that "we are doomed!"

The Communist Manifesto makes it quite clear that, as a result of the industrial revolution, radical changes were established in society:

"The modern bourgeois society that has sprung from the ruins of feudal society has not done away with class antagonisms. It has but established new classes, new conditions of oppression, new forms of struggle in place of the old ones.

"Our epoch, the epoch of the bourgeoisie, possesses however, this one distinctive feature: it has simplified the class antagonisms. Society as a whole is more and more splitting up into two great hostile camps, into two great classes directly facing each other: bourgeois and proletariat."

This is especially true now, as around the beginning of the twentieth century, capitalism reached the stage of monopoly, technically referred to as "imperialism".

The monopoly capitalists, the imperialists, are determined to crush any competition, no matter how insignificant. As a result of this, the small time capitalist, which is to say the middle class small business owner or "petty bourgeois", has largely been wiped out, at least in the most highly industrialized countries of the world. The same is true of the family farmers, otherwise known as "peasants".

That brings us to the "intellectuals and salaried personnel" of the capitalists. Lenin says that they "correspond to the middle class". They tend to lead lives of "quiet desperation", waiting for the "axe to fall". Regardless of how well they do their job, they are well aware of the fact that the capitalist may fire them at any time, for any reason, or for no reason. "Because they can"!

The Communist Manifesto goes on to state:

"Modern industry has established the world market...and in proportion as industry, commerce, navigation, railways extended, in the same proportion the bourgeoisie developed, increased its capital, and pushed into the background every class handed down from the middle ages.

"We see, therefore, how the modern bourgeoisie is itself the product of a long course of development, of a series of revolutions in the modes of production and exchange.

"Each step in the development of the bourgeoisie was accompanied by a corresponding political advance of that class....

"The bourgeoisie, historically, has played a most revolutionary part.

"The bourgeoisie, wherever it has got the upper hand, has put an end to all feudal, patriarchal, idyllic relations. It has pitilessly torn asunder the motley feudal ties that bound man to his 'natural superiors', and has left remaining no other nexus between man and man, than naked self interest, than callous 'cash payment'. It has drowned the most heavenly ecstasies of religious fervour, of chivalrous enthusiasm, of philistine sentimentalism, in the icy waters of egotistical calculation. It has resolved personal worth into exchange value, and in place of the numberless indefeasible chartered freedoms, has set up that single, unconscionable freedom – free trade. In one word, for exploitation,

"The bourgeoisie has stripped of its halo every occupation hitherto honoured and looked up to with reverent awe. It has converted the physician, the lawyer, the priest, the poet, the man of science, into its paid wage labourers.

"The bourgeoisie has torn away from the family its sentimental veil, and has reduced the family relation to a mere money relation…It has accomplished wonders far surpassing Egyptian pyramids, Roman aqueducts and Gothic cathedrals; it has conducted expeditions that put in the shade all former exoduses of nations and crusades

"The bourgeoisie cannot exist without constantly revolutionizing the instruments of production, and thereby the relations of production, and with them the whole relations of society…

"The bourgeoisie has through its exploitation of the world market given a cosmopolitan character to production and consumption in every country…

"The bourgeoisie, by the rapid improvement of all instruments of production, by the immensely facilitated means of communication, draws all, even the most barbarian, nations into civilization…

"The bourgeoisie.. has created more massive and more colossal productive forces than have all preceding generations together…

"We see then: the means of production and of exchange, on whose foundation the bourgeoisie built itself up, were generated in feudal society…the feudal relations of property became no longer compatible with the already developed productive forces…they were burst asunder…

"Into their place stepped free competition, accompanied by a social and political constitution adapted to it, and by the economical and political sway of the bourgeois class."

I have chosen to quote the Communist Manifesto at length, partly because it is so important, and partly to drive home the point that *at one time*, the bourgeoisie played a most revolutionary role!

WORLD SOCIALIST REVOLUTION

Such is no longer the case! As soon as capitalism reached the stage of monopoly, which is technically referred to as "imperialism", the monopoly capitalists, the bourgeoisie, became completely *counter revolutionary*, referred to as "reactionary". Lenin documented this supremely well in his book, Imperialism, the Highest Stage of Capitalism.

These days, with the bourgeoisie so completely reactionary, we tend to lose sight of the fact that, at first, the capitalists were truly revolutionary! But to paraphrase an old and tired expression, "that was then and this is now"!

The Communist Manifesto goes into this in more detail:

"Modern bourgeois society with its relations of production, of exchange and of property, a society which has conjured up such gigantic means of production and exchange, is like the sorcerer, who is no longer able to control the powers of the nether world whom he has called up by his spells. ...It is enough to mention the commercial crises that by their periodical return put on trial, each time more threateningly, the existence of the entire bourgeois society...an epidemic of over production..."

The industrial revolution made possible, for the first time in history, the chance to provide for the well being of countless people. Everyone has a chance to benefit from this vast surplus! But as long as the monopoly capitalists are in charge, that is not about to happen! It would never occur to them to provide for the common good! They are completely focused on their "bottom line", which is the very thing they call their sacred *profit*!

Yet under capitalism, a "vast surplus" gives rise to "an epidemic of over production", a "crisis in capitalism". It threatens their profits! As a result, even less is available for the common people!

That is the "one side of the coin", so to speak. Scientific socialists may say that this is but "one aspect of the contradiction". The "flip side of the coin", or the "other aspect to the contradiction", is the fact which is stated quite clearly in the Communist Manifesto:

"The weapons with which the bourgeoisie felled feudalism to the ground are now turned against the bourgeoisie itself

"But not only has the bourgeoisie forged the weapons that bring death to itself; it has also called into existence the men who are to wield those weapons – the modern working class – the proletarians."

The fact of the matter is that as capitalism becomes ever more highly developed, so too does the modern working class, the proletariat. At least here in North America, and probably in most other highly developed countries, the proletariat is quite highly cultured. The vast majority are literate, and either own computers, or some other "digital device", or at least have access to them. This makes it ever so much easier to raise their level of awareness. The capitalists have thoughtfully created the Internet. The least we can do is express our appreciation, by using it against them!

Those who have been paying even the slightest bit of attention to the news lately, are no doubt struck by the fact that women are now playing a vital role in the international working class movement.

In particular, a young woman in Iran was arrested and killed, by the "morality police", for the crime of "not wearing her hijab properly". Bear in mind that a "hijab" is a head scarf. The protests against such violent repression have spread across Iran, to all cities and towns, and even to remote areas. Videos from Iran show women dancing in the streets, waving their head scarfs, burning those same scarfs and cutting their hair. These protests have spread to other countries, so that women in various countries are supporting their sisters in Iran.

The Communist Manifesto helps to explain this also:

"The more modern industry becomes developed, the more is the labour of men superseded by that of women."

As ever more women become drawn into the work force, becoming proletarians, the more they become revolutionary. After all, it is the proletariat which is the most revolutionary class!

This infusion of "fresh blood" into the international working class movement is most welcome! No doubt many of these women have been "watching from the sidelines", so to speak, perhaps "marvelling at the stupidity of so many men". Or so I have been told!

Now those same women, those whom were formerly confined to the drudgery of housework, have "come into the work force", have become proletarians, and therefore revolutionary, and are making their voices heard.

The fact is that a great many working men are supremely well aware that most of our leaders, including our union leaders, are "in the pocket of the capitalists". Yet by and large, most men tolerate this.

By contrast, the women whom have recently entered the workforce, are not at all inclined to accept the "status quo". Now that they are workers, proletarians, they are becoming ever more politically active. They are a most welcome edition to the working class, a "breath of fresh air"!

Without doubt, here in North America, they are in the forefront of the working class movement.

This brings us to the current political situation, in which capitalism is definitely in a state of crisis. The capitalists can no longer rule in the old way, and the working people are no longer content to be ruled in the old way. Lenin refers to this as a revolutionary situation.

Inflation is spiraling out of control, to the point that even the bourgeois economists are worried of a "repeat of the Weimar Republic", in which the value of the German mark depreciated, to the point that it was worthless. Those same economists are also openly speaking of a recession, while as yet, avoiding any mention of a depression.

Gun violence is so common, it is not even documented, unless four or more people are shot. Drug overdoses are now epidemic. The criminal gangs are in control of many neighbourhoods. Local police are reduced to documenting the crimes. A great many police officers are retiring or simply quitting. Very few people are even applying to join any police force, as "no one wants to become a cop". There are calls for "martial law" in some cities. It has been suggested that only the National Guard can "restore law and order".

From the viewpoint of the capitalists, the "cherry on the cake", is the fact that "one of their own", by whom they of course mean the former president, Donald Trump, is causing them untold grief! They just do not know what to do with that boy! He just will not shut up!

Recently, the New York Attorney General, NYAG, issued a two hundred page report, the product of a three year investigation. In that report, she alleges that Trump, along with three of his adult children, over a ten year period, submitted "fraudulent and misleading financial statements", on a regular basis. Accordingly, she is suing them for a minimum of 250 million dollars. Yet there are *no criminal charges! The government is afraid of Trump!*

In a very clear cut example of "passing the buck", she mentioned that the case had been referred to "federal prosecutors and the Internal Revenue Service", the IRS, for "possible federal crimes". By implication, all of those allegedly "fraudulent and misleading financial statements" failed to break any state laws! Not likely! She just dares not charge Trump!

If any working class person was suspected of committing such acts, especially that of *tax evasion*, then that person would likely never again see the light of day! Without doubt, there is a double standard here!

In fact, a federal judge admitted as much. The opinion she gave is a masterpiece of legal jibberish: "Based on the nature of this action, the principles of equity require the Court to consider the specific context at issue, and that consideration is inherently impacted by the position formerly held by the Plaintiff".

Now to put this in plain and simple English, she refers to herself as the Court, and to Trump as the Plaintiff. Her reference to her "consideration" of the "specific context at issue" which is "inherently impacted by the position formerly held" by Trump, is a reference to the fact that he was formerly the president. For that reason, she favoured Trump! So much for the courts being fair and impartial!

Clearly, the laws do not apply to the capitalists, only to the working people. No kidding! Yet this federal judge broke the "unwritten law" of all courts: Do not admit this!

Most members of the working class are well aware of the fact that the laws do not apply to the wealthy. Those who have enough money, are quite capable of buying themselves out of any criminal charges. There is no need to explain this to them!

By contrast, there is an urgent need to explain to the working people, the existence of classes. They must be advised, in terms they can understand, that those of us who work for wages are working class, "proletarians". The billionaires, monopoly capitalists, those who own almost everything of any great value, are members of a different class, that of the "bourgeoisie". Further, we are class enemies. The capitalists must be overthrown, the existing state apparatus destroyed, and the capitalists must be crushed, under the Dictatorship of the Proletariat. Yet who is to bring them this awareness?

The Communist Manifesto provides us with the answer:

"Entire sections of the ruling classes are, by the advance of industry, precipitated into the proletariat, or at least threatened in their conditions of existence. These also supply the proletariat with fresh elements of enlightenment and progress.

"Finally, in times when the class struggle nears the decisive hour, the process of dissolution going on within the ruling class, in fact within the whole range of old society, assumes such a violent, glaring character, that a small section of the ruling class cuts itself adrift, and joins the revolutionary class, the class that holds the future in its hands. Just as, therefore, at an earlier period, a section of the nobility went over to the bourgeoisie, so now a portion of the bourgeoise goes over to the proletariat, and in particular, a portion of the bourgeois ideologists, who have raises themselves to the level of comprehending theoretically the historical movement as a whole.

"Of all the classes that stand face to face with the bourgeoisie today, the proletariat alone is a really revolutionary class. The other classes decay and finally disappear in the face of modern industry; the proletariat is its special and essential product."

As I write this, the capitalists do not know "which way to jump". They are currently "counting down the days" to the midterm elections. Perhaps they think that a new Congress will solve all their problems!

The Democrats are fretting over losing control of the House or the Senate, while at the same time worrying that Trump will once again run for president, in the next federal election, two years from now. As for the revolutionary motion, they think perhaps the best way to divert it is with their "brainstorm" of "30×30". This is what Biden refers to as setting a goal of "conserving at least 30 percent of our lands and waters by 2030". Naturally, he was careful to not specify precisely what he meant by "conserve"!

This was pointed out in an excellent article of National Geographic. They provide an example of a farmer, a small time capitalist, who was quite happy to cooperate, to create"70 acres permanent wetlands", in the interests of conservation. Of course, that came with a government grant of "$350,000!" At taxpayer expense, of course! As the farmer stated, "it has to pencil out". By that rather strange expression, he meant that he was not about to sacrifice profit for wildlife. As long as the taxpayers are prepared to hand over money to small time capitalists, they in turn are happy to cooperate!

So much for the Democrats plan for "conservation"!

The Republicans are also "scratching their heads", trying to come up with something to counteract Trump and his "Make American Great Again, or MAGA". It should be noted that the keystone of the MAGA policy is to hold immigrants responsible for the horrors of capitalism.

The fact is that even the journalists, those faithful flunkies of the capitalists, are openly mentioning the possibility of civil war. It does not help that Trump recently issued a "thinly veiled threat" to that effect. He made it quite clear that if he is charged, his followers are prepared to take up arms!

The capitalists are taking him seriously! They are afraid of Trump! Each government agency is "passing the buck"! The state of New York is going after him for hundreds of millions which they say he owes them, while *documenting* countless instances of fraud and tax evasion, over the *last ten years*, but *not filing charges!*

It is clear that the capitalists are trying to discredit Trump, to expose him as a liar and fraud. That is by no means a "tall order", as that is precisely the case! In other words, Trump is a *typical* capitalist! The more they expose Trump, the more they expose themselves!

The capitalists are trying to turn "public opinion", as they phrase it, against Trump! Excellent! By a remarkable coincidence, we too are attempting to do the same thing! In this way, we can raise the level of awareness of the working class!

The capitalists are not about to face the fact – or are not capable of facing the fact? – that we are in the middle of a revolutionary situation. Yet even the journalists, those most devoted servants of the capitalists, now dare to mention this!

True, capitalism has reached a state of crisis. That is a fact. It is also a fact that the system will not collapse upon itself! So for those who think that the capitalists cannot find a way out of this mess, think again! As long as the proletariat does nothing, the capitalists will manage!

It is a fundamental tenet of Marxism, that all reactionaries are the same! They must be *destroyed*! They are not about to simply "fade away!" The capitalists are reactionaries, right to the very core of their being, and must be *crushed!*

It is the working class, the proletariat, and only the proletariat, that is up to this task. After all, it is only the proletariat that is the consistently revolutionary class. Yet that is not enough. Their level of awareness has to be raised. They need to be made aware of the existence of classes, of the conflict between the classes. Above all, they must be made aware of the necessity of Revolution and the subsequent Dictatorship of the Proletariat.

Contrary to what the demagogues may say, working people need leaders. *Proper leaders!* The only proper leaders are scientific socialists, Marxists, Communists!

The fact of the matter is that all classes have leaders, and that includes the capitalists. At the moment, one of the leaders of the capitalists is a fellow by the name of Donald Trump! He has quite a following, among the working people! But then, Trump is a first class demagogue!

Such people are not to be under estimated! Demagogues are the worst enemies of the working class! They have quite a following, among the proletariat, especially with the less advanced!

The less advanced workers are not to be blamed for this! They are under the influence of those who peddle the lies of the capitalists! They have been listening to such lies all their lives! Who can blame them for believing those lies?

These working people need to be told the truth. Further, it must be expressed in terms which they can understand. This is to say that we must use popular language, not "High English"! Feel free to use sports metaphors, but under no circumstances resort to vulgarity! Our goal it to raise their level of awareness, not to personally sink to a lower level.

Also, avoid the use of the word "backward". They may think that we are calling them "stupid".

There is no time to lose. The revolutionary motion is becoming ever stronger. Civil war could break out at any day. Now is the time to become active. Take part in the emerging Councils. Join the mainstream political parties, as card carrying members. Run for office. Flood Washington with Leftist people. Prepare for Revolution. Train in the use of weapons of all sorts. Give the capitalists no rest! Harass them in their homes, businesses, restaurants and resorts! Carry signs and banners which call for the Dictatorship of the Proletariat and Council Power!

Above all else, make every effort to raise the level of awareness of the proletariat. The working class must be made aware of itself *as a class!*

We will know we are being successful when working people are openly discussing Council Power and the Dictatorship of the Proletariat!

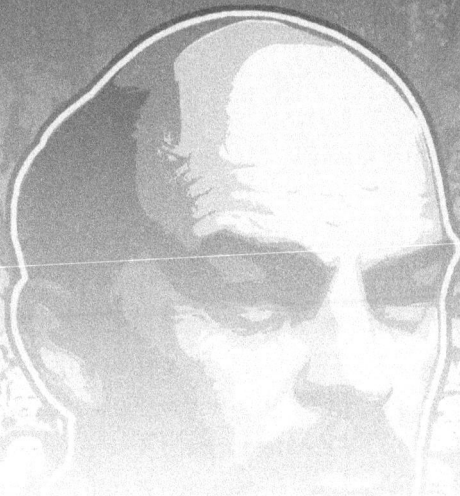

# CHAPTER 2

## Concerning the Ukraine War and Nuclear Weapons

October 20, 2022

On February 24, 2022, Russia invaded the neighbouring country of Ukraine. No doubt, the plan was to annex Ukraine, as part of the plan to restore the Russian Empire. After all, at the time of the Czars, Ukraine had been part of that Empire. Yet "right from the get go", things did not work out quite the way the Russian military had planned. The Ukrainians had other ideas!

As is well known, the Russian advance was stopped outside the capital city of Kiev, and then pushed back to the East. This came as a great surprise to the Russians. The military analysts of the world were equally surprised, as the invading armies of the Russians had an overwhelming advantage in artillery, aircraft and armour. Clearly, the military analysts have overlooked a few things.

There is a popular expression to the effect that "the military is busy preparing for the last war". True enough! The Russian invasion of Ukraine is very similar to the Nazi invasion of western Europe in 1939. At that time, their military doctrine of "blitzkrieg", or "lightning war", was put to the test. It succeeded, beyond all expectations! The highly industrialized countries of Western Europe were defeated, within a matter of months!

As the lead Nazi and the Chancellor of Germany, Hitler was deeply impressed by those early victories. In fact, he was so impressed that he "broke his own rule", that of "never fighting a war on two fronts", and decided to invade the then socialist Soviet Union.

I mention the fact that the Soviet Union was, at that time, a socialist country, for the benefit of those who are just now becoming politically active. The capitalists have since managed to restore capitalism in Russia. More on that subject, later on in this article.

The current Russian aristocracy, or billionaires, or "oligarchs", technically referred to as the bourgeoisie, have succeeded in setting themselves up as the "new Czars". Led by President Putin, they are determined to restore the Russian Empire, to "Make Russia Great Again"! As Ukraine was once part of that Empire, it is only natural for them to assume that they have the "God Given Right" to "reclaim" that country! Hence the invasion!

Yet even the Nazis were not so stupid as to invade the Soviet Union during "spring break"! That is a reference to the fact that the ground freezes solid during the winter, but thaws out in the spring. At that time, the ground becomes wet and soft, so that vehicles become "bogged down", as soon as they leave the paved roads. For that reason, the Nazis decided to wait until the ground dried out. Their invasion of the Soviet Union took place on June 22, 1941.

By contrast, Putin decided to ignore this fundamental fact of Nature, and in a display of mind boggling stupidity, sent his troops into battle at the beginning of spring break!

The Ukrainians, led by President Zalensky, were quick to use this to their advantage. The columns of Russian vehicles, which had planned to capture Kiev, were first immobilized on the paved roads. The lead vehicles were destroyed, and as the following vehicles were unable to turn around, they became "sitting ducks"!

The Ukrainians then "took the bull by the horns", and mobilized for full scale war! Most of the men who were of military age joined the military. A great many women took over the jobs which had been vacated. Others also joined the military. Most of the civilians were evacuated from the war zone, to the west and relative safety, or even out of the country. The factories were "geared up" for war production.

As well, a great many industrialized countries chose to send "technologically advanced" weapons to Ukraine, and to provide training for select troops. These weapons include portable rocket launchers and drones, as well as long range, accurate artillery pieces.

In particular, the rocket launchers have managed to neutralize the overwhelming advantage of Russian aircraft and armour. They have proven to be most effective in "knocking out" armoured vehicles, including tanks, otherwise known as "panzers", as well as aircraft, both helicopters and fixed wing.

They have found that the use of drones, in order to precisely locate the position of the enemy armour, has proven to be most useful. Used in combination with the portable rocket launchers, the results have been "most satisfactory"!

Of course, the drones are also useful, in and of themselves. They are able to carry explosives, if only light weight, but capable of doing considerable damage.

This is the very thing the military planners have overlooked! "High Tech"! During the Second World War, various armies had portable rocket launchers. For example, the German Panzer Faust was considered the best. Yet all were "short range" weapons, as well as not terribly accurate, so that their effectiveness was limited. Not so with the modern rocket launchers!

With modern technology, the rockets now have a considerably longer range, and can hit with "pinpoint precision"!

During the first few months of the war, the Ukrainian High Command was able to remove most civilians to positions of relative safety. As well, they were able to repulse the enemy attack on the capital, to "gear up for war", and to neutralize the Russian advantage in armour and aircraft. Yet the Russians still had a vast superiority in artillery.

Now that superiority has also been neutralized, due to the donation of a great many long range, high calibre, accurate artillery pieces, from other countries. The Ukrainians are using these weapons to great effect! Their drones are helping them to locate the enemy "storage sites", the place where the ammunition is kept, as well as the "communications centres". Then the long range artillery is destroying these key installations.

That has enabled the Ukrainians to go "on the offensive"! The latest reports are that they are scoring some major victories, regaining a great deal of territory, formerly occupied by the Russians.

Now Putin has responded by "annexing" parts of Eastern Ukraine, so that he claims they are now "part of Russia". He has also declared a "partial mobilization", so that an additional 300,000 troops are being drafted into the Russian army.

As I write this, it is early October, and the press is reporting that some of those "conscripts" have already appeared in Ukraine! These "soldiers" have little or no training! They are little more than "cannon fodder!" Has Putin gone mad?

This month also marks the beginning of the "wet season", in that we can expect heavy rain. Of course that too makes the ground soft, so that vehicles cannot travel off paved roads. This is to the advantage of the defender.

Further, the press is reporting that the Kerch Bridge, a 19 kilometre, or 12 mile bridge, which connects the Russian mainland to the Crimean Peninsula, has just been severely damaged. This event is of exceptional importance, for several reasons.

The Crimea was occupied by Russia in 2014. Then in 2018, the Kerch Bridge was built, at great expense, of course. Since the Russian invasion of February, it has served as a vital "artery", a "key supply route" for the war in Ukraine. This is referred to as "logistics", as the bridge provides a railroad as well as a highway. Vast amounts of military hardware were being transported by rail, far more so than by road. Now that flow has been reduced to a "trickle"!

As a consequence, the Russian army, located in southern Ukraine, is in serious trouble. The vast amount of equipment, which the army needs, is now in short supply.

Strangely enough, the Ukrainians have yet to take credit for the destruction of the Kerch Bridge. It is possible that a group of "Partisans", which is to say Ukrainian "freedom fighters", working "behind enemy lines" in the Crimea, were able to blow up that bridge. They may not have even been in contact with the Ukrainian High Command!

Whatever the cause of the destruction, it is also a major psychological victory for the Ukrainians! It does wonders for Ukrainian morale!

That is not the only "headache" for Putin.

The opposition of the Russian people, to the war in Ukraine, is now similar to the opposition of the American people, at the time of the war in Viet Nam. Protests are now taking place, across the country. The Russian authorities are responding with considerable brutality, beating and arresting protesters. As well, a great many young men are running to other countries, in order to avoid military conscription. This is commonly referred to as "draft dogging".

The working people of Russia must be supported in their opposition to the invasion of Ukraine. This is to say that their level of consciousness must be raised. They must be made aware of the fact that the capitalists have returned to power, that Russia is no longer a socialist country. It is now an imperialist country. It is once again necessary to overthrow the capitalists, the bourgeoisie, and crush them, under the Dictatorship of the Proletariat.

Russia has a fine Revolutionary history, of which they can be most proud! Russia is the home of Lenin! Russia is the country which overthrew the Czars! Russian is the country which first gave birth to Soviets! Russia is the country which overthrew the capitalists! Russia is the country which established the first socialist republic! Russia is the country which established the first Dictatorship of the Proletariat!

Russia is the country which did this once, and Russia is the country which will do this again!

At the time of the rule of the Czars, all revolutionary literature was banned. The common people had no democratic rights. Now that Putin and his henchmen are in charge, a similar situation has arisen. Once again, common people have no democratic rights, and all Marxist literature is also banned. So how to raise the level of awareness of the Russian working class? In much the same way that Lenin managed!

At the time of the Czars, Lenin was living in exile. Yet that did not stop him from smuggling in Revolutionary literature, with great difficulty, I might add. This served to raise the level of awareness of the Russian people, preparing them for the revolution. Now it is time for us to do the same thing! The only difference is that now, we can use the internet, the "electronic word"!

We can do our part to assist the next Russian Revolution, by emailing, in the Russian language, of course, Revolutionary literature, especially that of Lenin.

Bear in mind that it is not necessary to get in touch with each and every citizen of Russia. Working people have the utmost respect for the more advanced members of their class. They listen closely to such people. It is of the utmost importance that we focus on such workers. As Lenin stated, "It is only the class conscious minority that can direct and lead the broad masses of the workers".

For that reason, it is our duty, the duty of Communists, to raise the level of awareness of the most advanced strata of the proletariat of Russia. They must become "class conscious", aware of the revolutionary theories of Marx and Lenin. This includes the necessity of overthrowing the capitalists and smashing the existing state apparatus. As well, the terms

Soviet Power and the Dictatorship of the Proletariat, must become common place expressions.

Of course, it is not just the proletariat of Russia that requires revolutionary literature. The proletariat of other countries, especially those that are highly industrialized, also need to become class conscious. They too, need to become aware of the revolutionary theories of Marx and Lenin. The most advanced strata of the workers in all such countries must become true Communists, fighting for Soviet Power and the Dictatorship of the Proletariat. Of course, the best way to do this, is with a proper Communist Party, within each country.

Yet as we live in something other than an ideal world -no kidding, you say!- that is not always possible. In a country such as Russia, in which common people have almost no democratic rights, any attempt to create such a Communist Party would likely "backfire". That is a fact to which Lenin could testify!

It was Lenin who gathered together a number of middle class intellectual Marxists, in 1895, and formed the Russian League of Struggle For the Emancipation of the Working Class. All were promptly thrown into prison!

At that time, the Russian Secret Police had informers "everywhere"! These people, commonly referred to as "rats", are only too anxious to "rat out" their fellow citizens! Their only concern is with having their "palms greased"! Capitalism gives rise to such human filth! No doubt, Putin and his cronies are using such people to identify Revolutionaries, so that they too can be thrown in jail.

Lenin learned from his mistake, and it is hoped the current Russian Communists will also learn.

That is the "bad news", if you will excuse the tired old worn out joke. The "good news", so to speak, is that it is not necessary to form an official Russian Communist Party. As Lenin explained, writing after the Russian Revolution, ".... a minority that will fight resolutely for the Dictatorship of the Proletariat, and will educate the masses of the workers along these lines, then in reality this minority is nothing but a Party".

Without doubt, those who are aware of the Revolutionary theories of Marx and Lenin, and are prepared to "fight resolutely for the Dictatorship of the Proletariat", are definitely in a "minority". They are very likely middle class, petty bourgeois, or perhaps former members of that class. It matters not. As long as they are prepared to "educate the masses of the workers along these lines", and raise the most advanced members of the proletariat, to the level of "conscious people", Communists, then there is no need to go through the formality of forming a proper Communist Party. They already comprise such a Party!

The previous Russian Revolutions have revealed the fact that during a Revolution, or even immediately before a Revolution, Soviets appear! This just happens, quite spontaneously! Bear in mind that the Russian word Soviet means Council, in English.

It is reasonable to assume that these Soviets have once again taken shape, in Russia. No doubt, the most advanced workers are involved in these Soviets. After all, it is the most advanced workers who tend to be politically active.

Previous Revolutionary experience has also revealed that these Soviets tend to spread, to various parts of the population. This is to say that we can expect to see Soviets of Workers, as well as that of Peasants, and of the Military. The Soviets in the Russian Military may take the shape of Soldiers or Sailors, possibly both. The name they choose is entirely up to them. It is our duty to raise their level of awareness, as they are destined to play a key role in the approaching Revolution.

These Soviets first appeared in Russia, in 1905, at the time of the first Russian Revolution. They were also crushed in 1907, at the time of the crushing of the that Revolution. They reappeared at the time of the Second Russian Revolution, of 1917.

The difference was that the Soviets of 1917 Russia, were far stronger than the Soviets of 1905. This was a factor in removing the Russian nobility from power. Bear in mind that the Romanovs had been in power for *three hundred years!* Yet in February of 1917, within the space of a few short days, Czar Nicholas was forced to "kiss the throne good bye"!

With the nobility out of the way, the Russian capitalists were "in their glory"! This gave rise to the democratic republic, which is the "ideal political shell for capitalism", according to Lenin. A fellow by the name of Kerensky was placed in charge, so that it became known as the "Kerensky Regime".

The fact of the matter is that the abolishment of the Russian monarchy was a step in the right direction, but only a step. The common people of Russia were no longer being crushed by the nobility and the capitalists. At that point, they were "merely" being crushed by the capitalists! Not a vast improvement!

As previously mentioned, at that time, Lenin was in exile. Yet he managed to return to Russia, in April of 1917. To this day, bourgeois scholars wonder why the Russian authorities did not arrest him, as soon as he stepped off the train, in the capital of Saint Petersburg.

The answer is quite simple: *Because they could not!* The *Soviets were that powerful!*

The secret police of Kerensky certainly *wanted* to arrest Lenin. The "spirit was willing, but the flesh was weak", so to speak. Within the space of a very short time, the Soviets became strong enough to challenge the authority of the Kerensky government!

This is to stress upon people the *Power of Soviets!* They are not to be under estimated! In fact, shortly after their appearance in Russia in 1917, they were able to overthrow the government and establish political power! Focus on the Soviets!

Now to return to the subject of the war in Ukraine.

It is significant that Putin is now calling up his military Reserves. He was forced into this, as the Russian Army, in Ukraine, which formerly consisted of youngsters, has been effectively destroyed. Older men are now being mobilized, and they are by no means as reliable as an army of the younger generation. On the contrary, they are more open to the propaganda of scientific socialism.

No doubt, various Soviets have also appeared among these military personnel. Now it is a matter of identifying these Soviets and sending them the revolutionary literature. In the Russian language, and in electronic form, of course! That is so much easier than getting it to them in paper copies!

The Russian military personnel in Ukraine are not the enemy, just as the Russian common people are not the enemy. The enemy is the Russian imperialists. It is the duty of Communists to make that clear in all our propaganda.

The current situation is similar to that which existed during the First World War. At that time, revolutionary motion was taking place in various industrialized countries. That too, gave rise to Soviets, or Councils.

At such a time, as Lenin pointed out, "As long as it was (and inasmuch as it still is) a question of winning the proletariat's vanguard over to the side of Communism, priority went and still goes to propaganda work".

Now is the time of "winning the proletariat's vanguard over to the side of Communism", of doing "propaganda work"! It is not just the working people of Russia that have to be "won over" to the "side of Communism"! That applies to all working people, especially the proletariat of the most highly industrialized countries.

Without doubt, they have already appeared spontaneously, "popped up", in America, so it is clear that we are close to a Revolution. After all, it is only during, or immediately before a revolution, that these Soviets appear.

It was only *after* the Great October Socialist Russian Revolution of 1917, that a "seismic shift" appeared in the ranks of the most advanced workers. This is to say that within the most highly industrialized countries of the world, the most advanced strata of the workers grasped the importance of Soviet Power and the Dictatorship of the Proletariat!

There is a popular expression, to the effect that "seeing is believing"! The most advanced strata of the population, of the most highly industrialized countries of the world, were convinced that the Communists were right! They became convinced of this, because they could see the results! The first Russian Soviet Socialist Republic, the first Dictatorship of the Proletariat, persuaded them! The Communists had it right, all along!

At that point, in 1920, Lenin referred to the possibility of a "World Socialist Republic". There was a reason for his optimism!

Immediately after the end of the First World War, several highly industrialized countries were on the brink of Revolution. For example, a very powerful Council of Action appeared in Britain. This Council was nothing other than a Soviet.

Britain was not the only industrialized country which was close to revolution. Most notably, Germany and America were singled out by Lenin. He was convinced that if the Socialist Revolution took place in all, or even several of the highly industrialized countries of the world, then a World Socialist Republic would take shape.

Yet Revolution in those countries clearly did not happen, *at least not yet*! So what went wrong?

Naturally, the bourgeois scholars assure us that Lenin was mistaken, that his theories have been proven to be false. They further state that the Berlin Wall was the "last bastion of Communism", and with the fall of that Wall in 1989, the world was made "safe for capitalism"! *Nonsense!*

Of course, this is not too surprising, as that is precisely what the capitalists want to believe. After all, it is in the best interest of these bourgeois scholars, to tell their "lords and masters" precisely that which they want to hear! Rest assured, the billionaires want to believe that they have nothing to fear from Communism! Dream on!

In fact, the World Socialist Revolution was - temporarily! - sidetracked, by acts of *murder and bribery*!

In Germany, Karl Liebknecht and Rosa Luxemburg were murdered. In Russia, Lenin was murdered. Great revolutionaries murdered! As well, countless other revolutionaries were murdered, and not just in Germany and Russia! These acts of murder are still taking place, and not just to Communists! In America, in 1968, Martin Luther King was murdered, even though he was a pacifist.

This is to drive home the point that it is necessary to take reasonable precautions, especially in the most highly industrialized countries. Those countries which have embraced imperialism, will not hesitate to murder any such leaders! In such cases, it may be best to "keep a low profile". May I suggest posting articles on the internet, but anonymously. Send these articles to select members of the working class, especially members of Soviets, or Councils. Make the government agents "earn their pay"! If the sex offenders and pedophiles can escape detection, then so can we!

The use of bribery is even more widespread than the use of murder. The fact of the matter is that the billionaires tend to keep a million or two on hand, in the form of cash, for "incidentals". As far as they are concerned, this is mere "spare change"! It has proven to be most useful in "pacifying" those who "cause trouble"! A little "palm greasing" goes a long way!

The fact is that working people need leaders. Proper leaders! People of principle! People who are not about to accept the bribes of the capitalists! People who are not about to be intimidated! Leaders who are going to tell common people the unvarnished truth, no matter how unpleasant! Leaders who are going to raise their level of awareness, to prepare them for Soviet Power and the Dictatorship of the Proletariat! Communist leaders!

Previous Revolutions, especially in the countries of Russia and China, can teach us a great deal. In particular, the mistakes of previous great Revolutionary leaders can be most instructive.

In the Soviet Union, the capitalists were able to return to power, after the death of Stalin. For that reason, the Chinese

Communists conducted a criticism of Stalin. They concluded that Stalin was a great Revolutionary, but committed a number of mistakes. It was these mistakes that allowed the Russian capitalists to return to power.

Years later, after the death of Mao, a similar situation took place. There too, the Chinese capitalists were also able to return to power. This was due to the fact that Mao was a great Revolutionary, but he too made some serious mistakes. This allowed the Chinese capitalists to return to power.

Both Russia and China are now, once again, capitalist countries. As I have covered this in a previous article, there is no need to repeat it here.

We must learn from the mistakes of previous great Revolutionaries! Everyone is human, so that we all make mistakes! As long as the mistakes are minor, and quickly corrected, that is not a problem, according to Lenin. Yet when the mistakes are major, and not corrected, then it becomes a huge problem!

Yet it was not just Stalin and Mao who made several serious mistakes. Under the Dictatorship of the Proletariat, it is the Members of the Central Committee, of the Communist Party, who are the closest adviser to the leader of the country. It is their duty to point out such mistakes! This never happened! In each case, the members of the Central Committee were negligent in their duty!

To return to the current situation, that of the Ukraine War, it is now that Putin has issued "thinly veiled threats", to the effect that he may use nuclear weapons. In response to this, President Biden has issued his own "proclamation" as to the possibility of "nuclear armageddon".

I should mention, for the sake of those who are just now becoming politically active, that weapons which are variously referred to as atomic, nuclear or thermonuclear, are basically the same. They are explosive devices which release a blast of extremely high heat, as well as radiation. For the purposes of this article, I refer to them as "nuclear" weapons. In popular jargon, these weapons are referred to as "nukes".

Without doubt, these weapons create terrible destruction. The experience of Hiroshima and Nagasaki are absolute proof of that! Which is not to say that it will mean the "end of the world"! The devastation of those two Japanese cities was terrible, partly because most of the homes were made of wood. By contrast, the buildings in most modern cities are made of brick and steel. A nuclear explosion in such a city – God Forbid! – would not create a firestorm. The damage would be confined to a rather small part of the city.

There are a great many scientists who are of a different opinion. They are a most vocal bunch, and have been preaching "Armageddon" for many years.

I will also mention that "Armageddon" is a biblical reference to the "place where the last battle between good and evil will be fought".

These "Doomsday Prophets" first got together in 1947, and created a "Doomsday Clock"! It has been maintained ever since, by the "Atomic Scientists", and this Clock is a "symbol that represents the likelihood of a man made global catastrophe". They further state that "the Clock is a metaphor for threats to humanity from unchecked scientific and technological advances".

They have a point! The key work here is "unchecked"! The monopoly capitalists, those who are technically referred to as "imperialists", are in charge, and they are fully prepared to use any and all means to maintain that power! The First World War has proven that, beyond any shadow of a doubt!

As well, they have used nuclear weapons before, in the Second World War, and they will not hesitate to use them again!

In fact, during the American war in Viet Nam, President Johnson and his military advisers gave serious consideration to the use of such a weapon. It was at the time of the battle of Khe Sahn, in 1968, and the American base was in danger of being over run. They considered "nuking" the Vietnamese! So what stopped them?

Historians would have us believe that "cooler heads prevailed"! By this stilted expression, they mean that American imperialists thought that the use of nuclear weapons would be a mistake. They were afraid that it would give rise to "wide spread protests", not only in America, but around the world! They refer to this as "public opinion" being "opposed to the use of nuclear weapons"!

The decision, of the American imperialists, to *not* use nuclear weapons, was *not* based upon any *moral* ground, but strictly because of the fact that the common people were dead set against it! The American imperialists were afraid that the use of such a weapon would trigger a rebellion, a *Revolution*, and that they would be "removed from power"!

This has not stopped a great many journalists from speculating on the "possibility" that "Putin is serious", that he may in fact "resort to nuclear weapons". Of course he is serious! Putin is a *typical* imperialist! The only question is, will the strength of the common people stop him?

Yet the Doomsday Prophets make no allowance for this!

The Doomsday Clock is currently set at "one hundred seconds to midnight". Those scientists would have us believe that at "midnight", which is to say that at the time of "nuclear war", the "vast majority of humans would die from burns, radiation and starvation. Human civilization would collapse!

Survivors would eke out an existence on a devastated, barren landscape."

Now that sounds pretty grim! Fortunately, it is simply not true! In fact, it is a pack of lies! The use of nuclear weapons is not to be confused with the "End Time", or "Armageddon"!

The scientists are presenting nuclear weapons as something which has the power of God! Such is not the case! If they have their way, we will all be kneeling down, worshiping "The Bomb"! That is not about to happen!

That begs the question: Why do they want us to worship "The Bomb"?

Marx provided us with the answer, when he stated that "religion is the opium of the people", used for "the exploitation and stupefaction of the working class".

The scientists, especially those who are responsible for the Doomsday Clock, are dedicated, hard working servants of the capitalists. They are trying to demoralize the working class, the common people. If they have their way, we will all be apathetic, taking no interest in politics, as the world will soon "come to an end"! What is the point of doing anything, if the world has no tomorrow?

Precisely what the capitalists want!

Perhaps working people can take inspiration from the Ukrainian people. They are now calmly facing the possibility that the Russians may use nuclear weapons against them, and discussing the various ways to deal with the resulting heat and radiation. The thought of "surrender" is not even being mentioned!

The Ukrainians deserve a great deal of credit! Throughout the course of the war, they have consistently out maneuvered the Russian invaders! They refuse to be intimidated by the threat of nuclear weapons!

In conclusion, we can now say that it is necessary for the working class to "recover some lost ground", to put it in military terms. The level of awareness of the working class must be, once again, raised to a higher level. The most advanced strata of the proletariat, the vanguard, must embrace Soviet Power and the Dictatorship of the Proletariat. This calls for a great deal of propaganda work. Communists must send Marxist literature, through the internet, to everyone, especially the most advanced workers. They must also become active in Soviets, Councils, as the most advanced workers will be found there. Take part in protests and demonstrations. Carry signs and posters which call for Soviet Power and the Dictatorship of the Proletariat. Harass the capitalists at their corporate and banking headquarters, as well as at their homes, restaurants and resorts. Give them no peace! Attract the press! Take videos and post them on the internet! With any luck, they may go "viral"!

Then too, so many common people are of the opinion that "seeing is believing". Such people should be encouraged, whenever possible, to become politically active. They should run for Parliament and Congress, for example. In countries such as Britain and America, such actions are allowed. Flood the various capitals with "Leftist" people! In this way, they will learn, from their own experience, that the billionaires, the bourgeoisie, are in charge, and fully intend to remain in charge!

Of course, in other countries, where citizens are allowed almost no democratic rights, such as Russia, that is out of the question. In such cases, propaganda is the rule, along with deception and secrecy.

In this way, we can best support the people of Ukraine in their war with the Russian imperialists. At the same time, we are supporting the people of Russia, in their preparation to overthrow their capitalists. Further, as soon as Soviet Power and the Dictatorship of the Proletariat is established in several of the most highly industrialized countries, then we can once again consider that which Lenin foresaw, a World Socialist Republic.

Bear in mind that the Soviet Union did not immediately take shape. At first, after the Great October Socialist Revolution, it was just the Russian Soviet Socialist Republic. The various republics which had been crushed by the Czars, the Russian Romanovs, were granted independence. The people in those republics had no reason to trust any Russian! It took some time for those people to become convinced that Lenin and the Communists really meant what they said.

It was not until 1922 that four independent Soviet Socialist Republics came together, to form the Soviet Union. This was the Union of the Russian Soviet Federative Socialist Republic, the Ukraine Soviet Socialist Republic, the Byelorussian Soviet Socialist Republic, and the Transcaucasian Socialist Federative Soviet Republic. By the end of World War 2, the Soviet Union had expanded to include fifteen Republics.

It is important to note that each Republic was Socialist, and formed of Soviets. We can expect these Soviets, or Councils, to also take control of state power, here in the Western World. At that time, we can also expect to see that which Lenin foresaw in 1920:

World Socialist Republic!

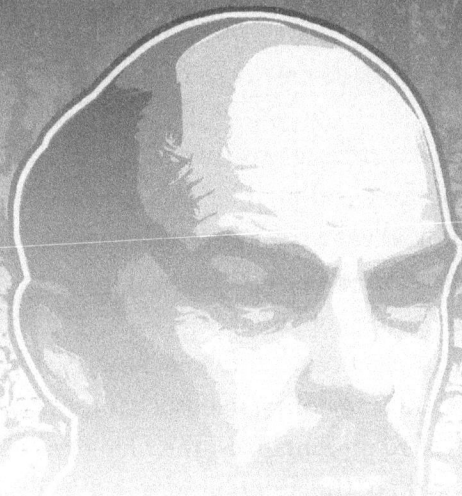

# CHAPTER 3

## Midterm Elections Countdown

It is now late October, and the "countdown" is taking place, as the journalists are counting the days to the 2022 "midterm elections", of November 8.

These elections are referred to as "midterm", because they take place in the middle of the four year term of the presidency. The last presidential election was in 2020, and the next one is scheduled for 2024.

There are only two mainstream political parties in the country, Republican and Democratic. The Republican Party is frequently referred to as the "GOP", or Grand Old Party.

As well, Trump coined the slogan of Make America Great Again, or MAGA. He has a considerable following, to this day.

The Democratic Party won the presidency in 2020, so that Biden is now president.

The country also has a Congress, in the form of the House of Representatives, and a Senate. The House has 435 members, and each Member serves a two year term, so that all House Members are up for election. The Senate has 100 Members, and each Senator serves a six year term. One third of the Senators run for election, every two years. This year, thirty five Senate seats are being contested.

As a result of the 2020 election, the Democratic Party was able to secure a "razor thin" majority, in both "Houses of Congress". In the House of Representatives, the Democrats have ten more Members than the Republicans, while in the Senate, it is evenly split, 48-50, with two "Independent Senators", who generally vote with the Democrats. Yet as the Vice President is the President of the Senate, and also a Democrat, she is able to cast the "tie breaking vote".

The "political pundits", or "election watchers", are deeply concerned with the possible outcome of the forth coming midterm election. They take great delight in stating that during the midterm elections, the "Party in power" generally loses some seats in Congress. If that happens this election, then the "Republicans will seize control of both Houses of Congress".

They further predict that, if that happens, the government will be effectively "deadlocked".

Certain of the journalists are starting to sound more like "doomsday prophets", rather than journalists. In referring to the GOP candidates who embrace MAGA, they are using such expressions as "a five alarm fire for democracy", that their anticipated election will be the "beginning of the end of American democracy". They are also afraid that the "midterms could slip into chaos"!

Their reference to "slipping into chaos" reveals the real reason for their concern. They are afraid that the "midterms" could lead to full scale civil war! The Second American Revolution!

Incidentally, I tend to pay attention to the facts that the more progressive journalists state, rather than their opinions. They are generally able to accurately gauge the degree of discontent of the public.

The more progressive journalists are concerned that, across the country, there are 300 GOP candidates, who "think that the 20-20 presidential election was stolen." This is to say that they are supporters of Trump, 'MAGA people", those who think that Trump is the true president! The fear is that if enough of them are elected to political office, there is "no telling what could happen"! Their fears are well grounded!

It is likely that the journalists are including the candidates for governors of various states, within that 300 number.

In particular, the journalists are focused on the gubernatorial election in the state of Arizona. The "GOP" candidate is a lady by the name of Kari Lake. In all fairness, she is young and attractive, or "easy on the eyes", to put it in popular terms. The journalists describe her in somewhat different terms.

As far as they are concerned, she is "Donald Trump in Heels", the "most dangerous candidate in America", a "threat to our democracy", a possible 2024 "running mate to Trump". It is safe to say that the journalists are not a "member of her fan club!"

They go on to say that she is "smart and savvy", a "performer", "uniquely dangerous", has "charisma", has adopted a "cynical but successful strategy". Allegedly a former democrat, and supporter of Obama, they maintain that she "switched sides, when it was convenient to do so".

They point out the fact that Kari Lake was formerly a "tv anchor", so that she is comfortable in front of a camera. Her harshest critics also maintain that she is able to "read the room", able to "take the temperature" and gauge the "anti media sentiment". Clearly, the journalists are accusing her of being not only beautiful, but also brilliant! Beauty and brains, a rare combination!

In her own words, "People do not trust elections since 2000." She is right about that! She is also aware that people "do not trust the media"! That too is true! For that reason, she has turned against the media! Even though she was recently part of that media! She has turned against her own people!

Such people are referred to as "opportunists", which is to say that they are completely devoid of principle. They are strictly "one way", their way, out for themselves. They have no sense of loyalty, prepared to do "whatever it takes" to "get to the top". No wonder the journalists are so afraid of her!

There is a fine chance that Kari Lake will soon be elected governor of the state of Arizona. When asked if she is prepared to accept the result of the election, she allegedly stated that she is fully prepared to accept the election results, "as long as I win". Spoken like a true follower of Trump!

Yet the journalists are also concerned with the fact that, in two other states, there are also "MAGA" candidates for the office of governor. No doubt they are concerned that this may constitute a trend.

The journalists are accusing those MAGA candidates of being fascists! That is a strong accusation! The journalists are afraid that if enough of them are elected to office, it will mean the "end of democracy"!

For the sake of all those who have just recently become politically active, I will mention that fascism is defined as a

"Far right, authoritarian, ultra nationalistic political ideology and movement".

Bear in mind that the opinions of the journalists, are just that, personal opinions, and are not based on any scientific belief. It is important to place the current political situation in correct scientific context, rather than in the opinions of various people.

From a scientific viewpoint, it is more accurate to describe these MAGA people as reactionaries. By definition, such a person, "holds political views that favour a return to the status quo, the previous political state of society, which that person believes possessed positive characteristics absent from contemporary society."

With that in mind, we can state that early capitalism was competitive, and possessed certain progressive characteristics. That all changed dramatically, around the beginning of the twentieth century, when capitalism reached the stage of monopoly, referred to as "imperialism".

It was Lenin who conducted a scientific investigation of imperialism. That investigation is included in his excellent article, Imperialism, the Highest State of Capitalism. HIs conclusions can be summarized as follows: "Imperialism, which means the partition of the world and the exploitation of other countries besides China, which means high monopoly profits for a handful of very rich countries, creates the possibility of corrupting the upper stratum of the proletariat, and thereby fosters, gives form to, and strengthens opportunism." He goes on to say that "the political features of imperialism are *reaction all along the line*". (my italics)

Without doubt, the opportunists must be fought. That includes the leaders of the MAGA movement, those who are the strongest supporters of Trump. As well, the "upper stratum of the proletariat", those who have been "corrupted" by capitalism, which is to say those who have accepted the bribes of the capitalists, must be opposed. That does *not* include the vast majority of working people, many of whom have embraced the MAGA ideology.

We must be careful to distinguish between the MAGA leaders, as opposed to their followers, the broad mass of common people, the "rank and file".

The revolutionary motion, which is currently sweeping the country, has succeeded in rousing a great many people to political activity. Those who were formerly apathetic, are now "waking up", as they phrase it, and questioning everything they have been told, all their lives. Excellent!

True, many of these people are now being misled, so that they have embraced the lies of the MAGA people. These lies include the "invasion of America at the southern border"! As if immigrants are the problem! They most certainly are not! The capitalists are the problem! Now it is a matter of making working people aware of that!

With that in mind, may I suggest we face the fact that the MAGA people claim that the 20-20 presidential election was fraudulent. They insist that Trump really won the election, that he is the true president.

They have a point! The 20-20 presidential election was fraudulent, but not for the reasons that they state. It was fraudulent because it was Unconstitutional! As I have covered that in a previous article, I will not go into that here.

The journalists are further convinced that the state of Nevada is "Ground Zero" for this upcoming revolt. Strangely enough, they give no reason for this belief.

They maintain that there are "forty four counties in fifteen states" which may well elect "Election Deniers", those who

WORLD SOCIALIST REVOLUTION

are convinced that Trump is the true president. If elected, they could well "replace local government leaders" and "throw out the election results"!

In other words, they could deny that Biden is president! They could further recognize Trump as president! In fifteen states, no less! That is the very definition of Revolution!

The journalists consider this to be a "threat to democracy"! They are so right! It is a threat to the *democracy of the capitalists!*

As we live under capitalism, it is the *capitalists* who rule! The *monopoly capitalists! The imperialists! The billionaires!* These are members of a class of people referred to as the bourgeoisie!

By contrast, we have a class of people who work for wages, working class people, referred to as proletarians. The democracy of the capitalists, referred to as "bourgeois democracy", is nothing other than a dictatorship, over the proletariat.

It must be explained to working people that democracy is a *method of class rule!* It is *not majority rule!*

As we live under capitalism, it is the *class of capitalists* who are in charge! It is democracy for the billionaires, but a *dictatorship* over the working people, the *proletariat!*

As for those who are skeptical, may I suggest that you *wake up!* Watch the news! Almost everyone, even the government officials, admit that Trump is guilty of countless crimes. Yet there is no mention of charging him! Trump is a billionaire! Trump can do what he wants! And he does! They all do! Trump is not exceptional! Trump is *typical!* The laws do not apply to billionaires!

Lenin covers this supremely well in his excellent article, State and Revolution. It is up to the working class, the Proletariat, to overthrow the capitalists, smash the existing state machine, that which has been set up to crush the working class people, and set up a new state apparatus, to crush the capitalists, under the Dictatorship of the Proletariat!

The capitalists have reason to be concerned. The official "approval rating" for Biden is now at 44 percent. Inflation has "sky rocketed", so that the cost of living has "gone through the roof". Even the International Monetary Fund, the IMF, is warning that the "worst is yet to come". They are predicting a *"global recession!"*. As yet, they dare not use the dreaded "D word", that of Depression.

Of even more concern to the capitalists, is the fact that ever more working people are becoming politically active. In various states, early voting is already taking place, and a "record turnout" is being reported. This is an indication that working people are no longer apathetic.

The journalists are also reporting that "the public no longer trusts any election results". Worse, "the public no longer trusts the media"! With good reason, I might add! The journalists are in the service of the capitalists! The capitalists have every reason to be worried!

It is not just in America that people are in revolutionary motion. In Britain, the latest Prime Minister was in power a mere six weeks, before being forced to step down. In Iran, there are massive protests. Most of the highly industrialized countries of Europe are in turmoil. The anti-war movement is raging in Russia. Inflation is causing the standard of living, of all working people, to drop dramatically. The world wide "recession", as predicted by the IMF, is about to intensify the suffering of all common people.

This is another way of saying that the situation is revolutionary, especially in highly industrialized countries, around the world. Working people are simply not about to tolerate much more from capitalism.

As soon as all, or even most, of the highly industrialized countries overthrow the capitalists, and establish socialism, in the form of the Dictatorship of the Proletariat, then indeed that will give rise to that which Lenin predicted:

World Socialist Republic

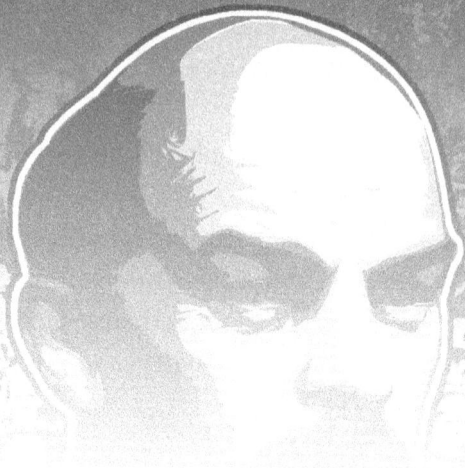

# CHAPTER 4

## Inflation and the Economy

The midterm elections are over, so that the public is relieved of the burden of listening to the constant political ads. At least for the moment. Yet it is very likely that the campaign for the next federal election, that of 2024, will begin very soon.

If nothing else, this midterm election has confirmed, that which everyone knew. The country is deeply divided!

Before the election, the Democrats controlled the presidency, as President Biden is a Democrat. They also had a "razor thin" majority in both "Houses of Congress", that of the Senate and the House of Representatives. Now that the midterm elections are over, it is still not clear which Party will control either House of Congress, as not all of the votes have been counted. It is clear that the "razor thin" majority will continue. Yet the Republicans may establish a majority, or "take control", of one, or both, Houses of Congress. That remains to be seen. We may not know for another month.

From our viewpoint, that of Communists, the final outcome is of little consequence, as both mainstream political parties, Democrat and Republican, serve the same class. That is the class of monopoly capitalists, the billionaires, the bourgeoisie. They do not serve the class of "common people", the working class, the wage earners, the proletariat. For that matter, they do not serve the small business owner, the middle class, the petty bourgeois.

I mention this for the sake of those who are just now becoming politically active, those who have recently "woken up". Welcome, my Brothers and Sisters, my Comrades!

I will also mention that I write these articles with the "little guy" in mind, the proletariat and the lower strata of the petty bourgeois. These are a few of the technical terms with which working people must become familiar. If we are not aware of these terms, the monopoly capitalists, the billionaires, the bourgeoisie, will use our lack of awareness against us.

The press is reporting that voter turn out was exceptionally high, especially for a "midterm election". This is excellent, as it indicates that countless people are politically active, taking an interest in their lives. In fact, it is characteristic of a Revolutionary situation.

The journalists have also done a fine job of documenting that which concerns the voters. Without doubt, it is the "economy" which "tops the list". This is to say that people are having a difficult time "making ends meet". The "cost of living" has gone "through the roof", and is continuing to rise, quite dramatically. In fact, inflation is at a forty year high.

As a result of this, common people are living "paycheck to paycheck". They are hard pressed to feed their families.

Many are relying heavily on canned food. Others are not so "fortunate". They are simply going hungry!

During the campaign, the Republican Party hammered the Democratic Party on various issues, especially that of the "economy", including "high inflation". In response, the Democratic Party harped on the issue of "democracy".

The journalists were openly wondering if the Democrats were *trying to lose the election!* After all, the voters were concerned with inflation, crime, immigration and abortion, and the Democrats *remained silent* on these issues! Instead, the Democrats kept repeating the *threat to democracy!*

As I have documented, in a different article, that democracy is nothing other than a method of class rule, there is no point in repeating it here.

I should add, by way of explanation, that I pay strict attention to that which the most successful journalists report. They do a rather fine job of documenting the facts. They listen to that which people say. On the other hand, I pay no attention to their analysis. After all, they are in the employ of the capitalists. It is in their best interests to "slant the news" in favour of the billionaires. For that reason, their conclusions are frequently in direct contradiction of the facts.

The fact is that the Democrats are now "caught between a rock and a hard place". As the Party in power, they cannot blame it "on the other guy", as is their first impulse. Nor can they tell the truth, which is that *inflation is characteristic of capitalism!*

Capitalists, by whom I mean the billionaires, are *ruled by greed!* They *worship money!* Those who have billions want more billions, and those who have hundreds of billions, want *thousands of billions!* They want to be *Trillionaires!*

In their pursuit of the almighty dollar, they deliberately create shortages. With their control of whole industries, they can do this. Frequently, I might add, and to great effect!

The most visible example of this is the high price of fuel. So many motorists cannot help but notice this when "filling up the tank". Yet that which is not so noticeable, is the fact that this high price of fuel serves to raise the cost of almost everything else.

The truck drivers have an expression: "If you bought it, we brought it". The point being that the trucks do not "run on love". They run on fuel. The higher the price of fuel, the higher the cost of delivering these goods, the higher the cost of the product. This is referred to as the "domino effect".

Of course, the capitalists have succeeded in creating a shortage in various other industries, including that of food for babies. There is no limit to the depths to which the billionaires are capable of stooping! That includes the starvation of infants, in their quest for the Almighty Buck!

Incidentally, monopoly capitalism is referred to as imperialism. Truly, when Lenin stated that "Imperialism is Reaction, right down the line", he was not joking!

Other issues, such as the fact that crime is out of control, as well as homelessness, immigration and abortion, are also "part and parcel" of capitalism. As such, the Democrats have also chosen to remain silent.

It may be objected that Biden, as President, has one tool he can use, to "tame inflation", which is that of raising interest rates. In fact, that is a common misconception. The President does not have that authority! Neither does the Congress! The interest rates, and in fact control of the economy, is in the hands of the capitalists, the billionaires! They exercise this control through the Federal Reserve!

Most working people are familiar with the expression, "He who controls the economy, controls the country"! There is some truth to this! It is more accurate to say that it is the *class* of people who control the economy, control the country! In our case, it is the *monopoly capitalist class,* the *class of billionaires,* the *bourgeoisie,* who have control of the economy. The *working class,* the *proletariat,* as well as the *middle class,* the *petty bourgeois,* have nothing to say about this!

As most common people are not aware of the existence of classes, I have chosen to use italics and repetition as a means of stressing this importance. It may help to think of this as being the first step on the road to class consciousness, to Revolution, to Soviet Power and the Dictatorship of the Proletariat. But then, I only say that because it is true.

This brings me to that which is commonly referred to as "High Tech". The capitalists have used that to great effect. Among other things, they have found it to be quite handy, when spying on us.

One good turn deserves another! The capitalists have also created personal computers and the Internet! Lo and Behold, we can use these most useful inventions against the capitalists! Most common people have computers, of one sort or another, or at least have access to them. For those of us who are in our declining years, the younger generation is a great source of assistance. After all, what are grandchildren for?

With that in mind, I turned to the Internet, to determine the role of "the Fed", as it is called. I stumbled upon this article, and was planning to document the key points. But then, as we have the technology, I decided to copy the whole thing. Behold:

"Is the Federal Reserve a privately owned corporation?

"September 2003

"Yes and no. The Federal Reserve (the Fed) enjoys a unique public/private structure that operates within the government, but is still relatively independent of government to isolate the Fed from day-to-day political pressures in fulfilling its varying roles. As stated in *The Federal Reserve System Purposes & Functions:*

"The Federal Reserve System is considered to be an independent central bank. It is so, however, only in the sense that its decisions do not have to be ratified by the President or anyone else in the executive branch of the government. The entire System is subject to oversight by the U.S. Congress…. the Federal Reserve must work within the framework of the overall objectives of economic and financial policy established by the government.

"History

"Prior to the Fed's formation, the United States experienced a number of economic downturns and financial panics. To help alleviate the problems associated with these swings in the economy, President Woodrow Wilson signed the Federal Reserve Act on December 23, 1913. The act's opening paragraph outlines its varying functions:

"An Act to provide for the establishment of Federal reserve banks, to furnish an elastic currency, to afford means of rediscounting commercial paper, to establish a more effective supervision of banking in the United States, and for other purposes.

"Since 1913, legislation has passed to augment some of the act's original purposes and to clarify the varying roles of the Fed.

"Structure

"Congress set up the Federal Reserve System to make it autonomous and to isolate it from day-to-day political pressures. For example, the members of the Board of Governors are appointed to serve 14-year terms that do not coincide with presidential terms. Key components of the Federal Reserve System are:

- The *Board of Governors*—Located in Washington, D.C., Board members are appointed by the U.S. President and confirmed by the U.S. Senate. Board members and staff are civil service employees.
- The *12 regional Reserve Banks*—Located around the country, the 12 Federal Reserve Banks are chartered as private corporations. Employees are not civil service.
- The *Federal Open Market Committee* (FOMC)—Composed of the Federal Reserve Governors and the Federal Reserve Bank presidents, the FOMC is charged with conducting monetary policy.

The 12 Federal Reserve Banks operate like other businesses; each has its own board of directors that selects the Reserve Bank president and first vice president, with approval from the Board of Governors. Each Branch of a Reserve Bank has its own board of directors. A majority of these directors are appointed by the Branch's Reserve Bank; the others are appointed by the Board of Governors.

"Boards of directors of the Reserve Banks and their Branches provide the Federal Reserve System with a wealth of information on economic conditions in every corner of the nation. The information, along with other sources, is used by the FOMC and the Board of Governors when reaching decisions about monetary policy.

"Key Responsibilities

"While Congress establishes key objectives the Fed must follow, the Fed generally works independently of the federal government to administer its core responsibilities.

"Those duties include:

- Conducting monetary policy
- Supervising and regulating banking and financial institutions
- Providing payments services to financial institutions

"The 12 Federal Reserve Banks have "independent" research staffs that advise their Reserve Bank presidents on monetary policy and the economy. Each Reserve Bank also has regulatory responsibilities including the supervision and regulation of financial institutions. The Reserve Banks also handle the Federal Reserve System's business operations—it is in this area that Reserve Banks operate more like private businesses, selling services like electronic funds transfers, check processing, and coin and currency services to financial institutions.

"Funding

"Congress also created the Federal Reserve System to be self-funding. The Fed earns interest on the interest-bearing government securities it holds in its portfolio and sells financial services to banks. This amount is reported each year in its annual report. The Fed's earnings typically far exceed its expenses. However, unlike for profit corporations, the Fed distributes any profit (after costs) to the U.S. Treasury. In 2002, the Fed's operating revenues were $26.7 billion, expenses total $2.2 billion, and $24.5 billion was paid to the treasury as "interest on Federal Reserve Notes."

(The items in italics were as copied from the Internet)

There we have it folks. In their own words, by their own admission, despite various qualifications, it is clear that the Fed is *independent* of the government. It is the *capitalists* who own and control the Federal Reserve, which is to say that the capitalists *control the economy!* No wonder the Democrats are silent concerning the economy! The economy is *out of their hands!*

Of course no politician is prepared to admit this! They would have us believe that under a democratic republic, *classes do not exist!* Such is hardly the case! Yet as the working class is not aware of itself as a class, the politicians are fully prepared to perpetuate the lie!

In fact, Lenin made it quite clear in his excellent article, What Is To Be Done?, that workers are not capable of becoming class conscious, by themselves. That awareness must be brought to the workers from an outside source. That outside source is middle class intellectuals. Lenin was one of those intellectuals.

The capitalists are also reluctant to admit the fact that they are capitalists! In fact, they avoid the word as they would the plague! But then, to admit that they are capitalists, is to admit that capitalism exists, so that classes exist!

Yet there can be no doubt that the working class is "making progress". Twenty years ago, at the time of the Occupy Movement, there was a vague awareness of difference, of "us" versus "them", of the "99 percent" versus the "1 percent". This is referred to as "class consciousness in embryonic form".

As those terms are no longer being used, it represents a step forward. Yet, as Lenin pointed out, "The history of all countries shows that the working class, exclusively by its own efforts, is able to develop only trade union consciousness". This is to say that working people may learn that "there is strength in numbers", as is indeed the case. That is about as far as it goes.

To become truly class conscious, aware of the existence of classes, and of the war between the classes, requires a knowledge of the works of Marx and Lenin. As workers are now quite cultured, most are perfectly capable of reading those works.

With that in mind, you may rest assured that nothing of substance will change, until the capitalists are overthrown. The state apparatus, which has been set up to crush the working people, must be destroyed and replaced by a Proletarian state apparatus, in order to crush the capitalists, as they strive to restore their "paradise lost". That new state apparatus is known as the Dictatorship of the Proletariat. It will be administered through Soviets, otherwise known as Councils.

We will know that we are on the right track, when working people are openly discussing Soviet Power and the Dictatorship of the Proletariat.

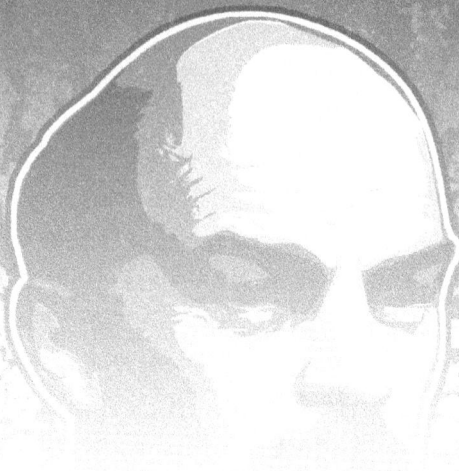

# CHAPTER 5

## Government Gridlock

It has been almost a week since the midterm elections, and yet we still do not know the identity of the mainstream political party which will take control of the House of Representatives. The votes are still being counted, in several states. The final result may not be known for several days yet, although it is very likely that the Republicans will take control, if only by the narrowest of margins. The Democrats have managed to maintain control of the Senate, also by the narrowest of margins.

The political pundits are scrambling to explain the reason the "red wave", which is the name they coined for the anticipated Republican overwhelming victory, has not materialized. Their idea of an "explanation" is to play the "blame game"! They are blaming the pollsters for producing false numbers, blaming the Republican Party leaders for poor leadership, and of course they are blaming their favourite "whipping boy", the press, for "leading them astray".

Some journalists are maintaining that the pollsters did not take into account the "Gen Z", in that Gen stands for Generation. According to the Internet, Gen Z is a reference to people born after 1995. while those born between 1980 and 1995 are referred to as "mellenials". These expressions are not mine.

The implication is that the younger generation is not at all impressed with either Party. With good reason, I might add. The fact that they are voting in "record numbers" is a good sign. It indicates that they are deeply dissatisfied, demanding change. Outstanding! To those people, I have but one word: Welcome! I am counting on you!

Donald Trump, the former president and unofficial leader of the Republican Party, was careful to cover all the bases, immediately before the election. At that time, he announced that in case of a Republican Party "red wave", he would take all the credit for success. On the other hand, in case of a defeat, he would accept none of the blame. Trump was not joking!

It is not too surprising that his main fury is focused against those who are possible threats to his authority, within the Republican Party. He has every intention of running for president again, in 2024, and is determined to eliminate any competition. In fact, the journalists expect him to announce his candidacy, within a week.

The Republican Party is in disarray. Their leader in the Senate, the Senator who was expected to be "promoted" from "Minority Leader" to "Majority Leader", is now under extreme pressure. Other Republican Senators are calling for his resignation, if only because they want his job.

The situation is little different in the House. The Republicans are currently a minority in the House, but may soon become the majority Party, if only by the narrowest of margins. In that case, the current House Minority Leader, a Republican, may soon become the official "Speaker of the House'". Yet the "rank and file" Republican members of Congress may stage a revolt, as they are not at all happy. They too are calling for new leaders.

The Democrats are in a similar situation. Most of the members of the Party are not satisfied with President Biden, especially as the polls indicate that his approval rating is "rock bottom". They too are looking for someone else to run for president in 2024. Yet clearly, Biden has other ideas!

Assuming the Republicans take control of the House, as is very likely, then we will have a "split government". This is to say that the Democrats still control the presidency and the Senate, but the Republicans control the House. This is exceptionally significant, if only because the *House controls the money!*

The journalists are reporting that the identity of the anticipated next Republican Speaker of the House, is a matter of no consequence, as they expect that the "Shadow Speaker of the House" will be *Donald Trump!*

Trump is the leader of the Republican Party, in everything but name! His word is law! The Republican Speaker of the House will "dance to his tune"! The result is sure to be government gridlock!

Bear in mind that on January 3, 2023, a new Congress will be sworn in. On that day, the 117 Congress will be dissolved, while the new 118 Congress will be sworn in. That gives President Biden and the Democrats a brief "grace period". They would be well advised to "use it wisely"!

In particular, the Treasury Secretary has warned that the American government will "run out of money on December

15". This is to say that on that date, the government will "reach the debt ceiling".

This business, that of "hitting the debt ceiling", has been going on for quite some time, so that the usual government response is to "kick the can down the road". This is to say that the House raises the debt ceiling slightly, so that the government can continue to operate for a short time, perhaps several months. Then they repeat the process.

Of course, the only reasonable thing to do is "balance the budget", as any citizen with any common sense can testify. That generally involves a combination of raising more revenue, and cutting expenses. Either that or bankruptcy!

As soon as the new Congress is sworn in, we can expect the Republicans to demand a "balanced budget". This could even happen before January 3, as the Congress currently in session is considered to be a "lame duck". It is entirely possible that they will choose to do nothing, even allowing the government to shut down on December 15. This is referred to as "passing the buck" to the new Congress!

Trump has made it quite clear that there is absolutely no way that the members of his capitalist class, that of the billionaires, the bourgeoisie, are about to pay any higher taxes. They pay very little tax now, and that is too much! That leaves the "common people", the working class, the proletariat, as well as the middle class, the petty bourgeois. Yet as they have been "bled white", it is clear that raising taxes on them is out of the question. It is simply not possible to "get blood out of a stone"!

The alternative is cutting expenses, and Trump is focused on the most obvious, that of Social Security and Medicare. These are the very programs that Biden is determined to protect! He is well aware that if he cuts those two social programs, his chances of being re-elected are negligible!

So on the one hand we have the President, who is terrified of an American bankruptcy. On the other hand, we have a former president who embraces bankruptcies! In fact, as one of his political opponents pointed out, his companies have declared bankruptcy on *six occasions!* The more Trump declares bankruptcy, the richer he becomes! He has a name for this! *Smart!*

Gridlock! The unstoppable projectile is about to meet the immovable object! The Republicans and Democrats are about to play a game of high stakes chicken! The Democrats are about to demand a raise to the national debt ceiling, while the Republicans are about to demand a "balanced budget", which will involve cutting social programs. At stake is the possible "default of the American government on the national debt"! In other works, bankruptcy!

The fact of the matter is that, since the days of the Civil War, the capitalists have managed to rule the country through the two Party system. Republicans and Democrats. Tweedle dee and Tweedle dum. Both serve the same class. Today, that class of capitalists is referred to as the billionaires, technically referred to as the bourgeoisie.

It is also a fact that the class of billionaires are completely reactionary. The one and only thing they care about is their profit, their "bottom line". It is never enough. In their quest for ever greater wealth, they do not hesitate to impoverish countless millions of people.

Even though the two Party system has served the capitalists well, for so many years, such is no longer the case. This is referred to as a "crisis in capitalism". It means that the old method of rule is no longer working, and the ruling class of billionaires will have to change their method of rule.

Bear in mind that there is nothing new and strange in this. Under capitalism, there is a continuous war taking place, between the ruling class of capitalists, and the class of people they rule and exploit, the working class, the proletariat. This class war is frequently hidden, but occasionally it flares up, in open rebellion. This open rebellion is referred to as Revolution. We are on the eve of an open Revolution, due in no small part to the "crisis in capitalism".

We have the experience of various Revolutions, under capitalism, so that we know what to expect. We can learn from that experience, including the mistakes of our ancestors, or we can choose to repeat those mistakes.

The Revolution which most closely resembles our own, is that of the Russian Revolution. In fact, there were no less than three Revolutions in Russia, in the early twentieth century. This provides us with a wealth of Revolutionary experience.

The first Russian Revolution of 1905, was completely spontaneous. Of necessity, I might add, as the Social Democrats, as the Marxist of the day referred to themselves, had all been thrown in jail, and were either killed or exiled. Lenin had been exiled.

That did not stop the Revolution, which proves that Marxists do not cause Revolutions. They merely provide leadership to Revolutions.

As is well known, the 1905 Revolution raged for two years. The unions went on strike, so that the factories were shut down. The railroads also quit running. The common people rose up and stormed the prisons, so that the inmates were released. The peasants stormed the homes of the landlords.

The pent up rage and frustration of countless working people was released!

For the first time in history, "Soviets" made an appearance. These Soviets, or Councils as they are referred to in English, began to "pop up" all over Russian, spontaneously, as a result of the Revolution. It is now clear that these Soviets are characteristic of Revolutions. They have currently made an appearance in America.

My point is that these popular uprisings happen, and on a regular basis. I refer to this as an Act of God. For those who do not believe in God, feel free to refer to it as an Act of a Higher Power.

The capitalist thought that this was terrible! They saw it as chaos and confusion! As the country was a monarchy, ruled by the Romanovs, the nobility was of the same opinion! They wanted nothing so much as to restore "law and order".

After two years, the Revolution died down, and reaction set in, as it always does, after an unsuccessful uprising. The capitalists were "in their glory". The trains were running once again, the factories were producing, and the capitalists were once again making money, which is about the only thing they really care about. Things returned to "normal".

Yet there had been a fundamental change, of which neither the nobility nor capitalists were aware. The common people, by whom I mean the workers and peasants, had just received a valuable lesson. They realized that the nobility and the capitalists were the enemy. Further, they were now veterans, experienced Revolutionaries.

It was several years before the Revolutionary motion picked up again. Yet "pick up" it did, and this gave rise to the second Russian Revolution of the twentieth century, in February of 1917. This second Revolution was far stronger and finer than the Revolution of 1905. The Soviets took shape once again. They had been crushed in 1907, at the same time the 1905 Revolution had been crushed, but now reappeared, only more powerful than ever.

As is well known, the February Revolution of 1917 succeeded in overthrowing the Czar, commonly referred to as Nicholas the Bloody. The capitalists then established a democratic republic, with Kerensky at the head. This became known as the Kerensky Regime.

The abolition of the monarchy was a step in the right direction, but only a step. The common people of Russia, by whom I mean the workers and peasants, were still suffering terribly. The country was still at war with the Central Power, including Germany. The people were cold and hungry. The peasants were denied the land they were promised, the Constituent Assembly was "delayed", and the butchery of the war continued. Not a great deal had changed.

The point is that the first two Russian Revolutions were spontaneous, and the working people had reached the limit of their ability. They had risen up, in magnificent style, and overthrown the Romanovs, those whom had ruled over them for *three hundred years!* They could go no farther!

There is a reason for this. As Lenin pointed out in his article, What Is To Be Done? "The history of all countries shows that the working class, exclusively by its own efforts, is able to develop only trade union consciousness". This is to say that workers have learned that there is "strength in numbers", as is indeed the case. For that reason, the more advanced workers gravitate towards trade unions, among other organizations, such as sports clubs. They then lobby for higher wages, working and living conditions. Occasionally, they are able to secure a paltry reform, if only temporarily. Yet nothing of substance changes!

Lenin goes on to say that "The theory of socialism, however, grew out of the philosophic, historical and economic theories that were elaborated by the educated representatives of the properties classes, the intellectuals. According to their social status, the founders of modern scientific socialism, Marx and Engels, themselves belonged to the bourgeois intelligentsia."

This brings us to the "theory of socialism", which was "elaborated" by the "founders of scientific socialism, Marx and Engels". It is clear that Lenin is careful to distinguish between the scientific socialism of Marx and Engels, and the "utopian socialism" of those who think that socialism is merely a "good idea".

Perhaps it would be best to hear that which Marx had to say on the subject:

"And now as to myself, no credit is due to me for discovering the existence of classes in modern society, nor yet the struggle between them. Long before me, bourgeois historians had described the historical development of this class struggle, and bourgeois economists the economic anatomy of classes. What I did that was new was to prove: 1) that the *existence of classes* is only bound up with *particular historical phases in the development of productions;* 2) that the class struggle necessarily leads to the *"Dictatorship of the Proletariat";* 3) that this Dictatorship itself only constitutes the transition to the *abolition of all classes and to a classless society."* (italics by Lenin)

This is to say that Marx studied the class struggle under capitalism. He further proved that it necessarily led to the "Dictatorship of the Proletariat", which is to say scientific socialism, as only under scientific socialism do we have the

Dictatorship of the Proletariat. This will in turn give rise to the "abolition of all classes" and in due time, to a "classless society".

It is significant that a great many people on the "Left", including those who consider themselves to be Democratic Socialists, are of the opinion that socialism is a good idea, but simply not possible. They are mistaken. On the contrary, it is not only possible, it is bound to happen! That is a fundamental tenet of Marxism! It is just a matter of time before the working class rises up, overthrows the capitalists, and crushes them, under the Dictatorship of the Proletariat.

Yet working people are not aware of this! Through no fault of their own, I might add. The Revolutionary theories of Marx and Lenin are not taught in school! At least, not in public schools! Mind you, they may well be taught in "Ivy League" Universities. They may be presented as "radical heresies", which have been "proven to be fraudulent". Or so they wish!

That in no way changes the fact that working people need leaders. It is up to those leaders to explain to the workers that the capitalists have to be overthrown and crushed, under the Dictatorship of the Proletariat. This is to say that the working class has to be made aware of itself as a class, with its own class interests.

In other words, it is up to the leaders to explain to workers, the Revolutionary theories of Marx and Lenin. That is the one and only way in which common people will learn, that at the time of the Revolution, it is necessary to overthrow the capitalists, and smash the existing state apparatus, that which has been used to crush the working people. It must be replaced by a new proletarian state apparatus, to be used to crush the "desperate and determined resistance" of the capitalists, as they try to "restore their paradise lost".

This new state apparatus is referred to as the Dictatorship of the Proletariat. It is to be administered through the newly created Soviets, or Councils.

To return to Russia, immediately after the February Revolution of 1917. As mentioned previously, the working people had gone as far as they could. Without leaders, scientific socialists, to give them direction, they could go no farther. In other words, they needed Lenin!

Without going into detail, Lenin was able to return from exile, in April of 1917. Of course, the secret police of Kerensky were anxious to kill him, on the spot! They were unable to do so, due to the strength of the Soviets! Within a very short time, these Soviets had become a power to rival the Kerensky government!

As the Czar had been overthrown, Lenin determined that it was necessary to overthrow the government of the capitalists, referred to as the Kerensky Regime. With that in mind, he wrote one of his greatest master pieces, State and Revolution.

Later that same year, on October 25, old style calendar, or November 7, new style calendar, the working people rose up and overthrew the government of the capitalists, the Kerensky Regime. This has gone down in history as the Great October Soviet Socialist Revolution. The first Soviet Socialist Republic was established.

The following three years were anything but "smooth sailing". Yet "against all the odds", the first Soviet Socialist Republic managed to survive. That provided Lenin with Revolutionary experience, which he was able to summarize in his excellent article, Left Wing Communism, An Infantile

Disorder. As it is of exceptional importance, I have decided to quote it at length:

"The fundamental law of Revolution, which has been confirmed by all Revolutions and especially by all three Russian Revolutions of the Twentieth Century, is as follows: for a Revolution to take place, it is not enough for the exploited and oppressed masses to realize the impossibility of living in the old way, and demand changes; for a Revolution to take place, it is essential that the exploiters should not be able to live and rule in the old way. It is only when the *'lower classes' do not want* to live in the old way and the 'upper classes' *cannot carry on in the old way* that the Revolution can triumph. This truth can be expressed in other words; Revolution is impossible without a nation wide crisis (affecting both the exploited and the exploiters). It follows that, for a Revolution to take place, it is essential, first, that a majority of the workers (or at least a majority of the class conscious, thinking and politically active workers) should fully realize that Revolution is necessary, and that they should be prepared to die for it; second, that the ruling classes should be going through a governmental crisis, which draws even the most backward masses into politics (symptomatic of any genuine Revolution is a rapid, tenfold or even hundredfold increase in the size of the working and oppressed masses -hitherto apathetic- who are capable of waging the political struggle) weakens the government, and makes it possible for the Revolutionaries to rapidly overthrow it." (italics by Lenin)

This was written in 1920, three years after the Great October Socialist Revolution. It is clear that a Revolutionary situation currently exists in America, as the "upper classes", the billionaires, can no longer "carry on in the old way". They are going to have to change their method of rule. It is also clear that the "lower classes", the working people, "realize the impossibility of living in the old way, and demand change".

Further, a "nation wide crisis" is imminent, as the country will soon face bankruptcy. Then too, Trump and his supporters may soon declare him to be president. As well, the country is set to break apart, into separate independent republics. As I have documented this in other writings, there is no need to repeat it here.

The only thing lacking is the fact that the majority of advanced workers are *not* aware that *"Revolution is necessary"*! That has got to change!

At the time that Lenin wrote this article, he was of the opinion that, among the industrialized countries of the world, the "most advanced strata of the Proletariat had embraced Soviet Power and the Dictatorship of the Proletariat". Such is no longer the case.

That is not cause for "doom and gloom" on our part. It just means that we "have our work cut out for ourselves". We have got to raise the level of awareness of the common people, by whom I mean the Proletariat and the lower strata of the middle class. We have got to bring their level of awareness to that of the working people of 1920. In that way, the country will truly be ready for Revolution.

The first thing we have to do is face certain facts, regardless of how unpleasant they may be. One fact is that there are a great many people who refer to themselves as Social Democrats, or a variation of those words. Yet none of them are endorsing the Revolutionary theories of Marx and Lenin. Either they are not aware of those theories, which is unlikely, or they are deliberately remaining silent on the subject. So be it!

For that reason, we cannot count on those people to help raise the level of awareness of the working class. So we will have to accomplish that task, without them. The working class is going to have to raise their own level of awareness. There is *no other way!*

Most working people, especially the most advanced, have computers, and know how to use them. The most important revolutionary works are available on the Internet, or at least can be bought through the Internet. In my opinion, State and Revolution is absolutely essential. As well, Left Wing Communism, An Infantile Disorder, is also supremely relevant. A careful reading of those two articles of Lenin, will go a long way towards that persons Revolutionary development. The two other articles of Lenin, which I consider to be vital, are Imperialism, the Highest Stage of Capitalism, and What Is To Be Done?

During the forth coming Revolution, working class leaders will emerge. Of that, there can be no doubt. Under capitalism, there are many people who have talent, but may not even be aware of the fact! As the Revolution rages, these people tend to "rise to the surface"! To such people, I can only say, do not deny your talent! Capitalism has given rise to countless liars! The last thing we need is another liar! That position has been filled, to overflowing! We need Proletarian leaders! Be honest with yourself! "To thine own self be true"! Do not be shy! Cultivate your talent! It will not blossom by itself!

In this article, I have focused on the federal elections, as so many working people are talking about this. In this way, it is hoped that their level of awareness will be raised.

The current situation is every bit as Revolutionary as it was in 1920. Perhaps even more Revolutionary, as the motion has now spread across North America, all of Europe and into Asia. As it is so much stronger and finer now, it is doubtful that the capitalists will be able to crush it through murder, intimidation and bribery, as happened in 1920.

At that time, Lenin foresaw a World Socialist Republic. The working people are doing their part. Now it is up to the most advanced workers to learn Scientific Socialism, which is Marxism. They can in turn carry that knowledge to the less advanced, so that all working people will be discussing Soviet Power and the Dictatorship of the Proletariat. In this way, the vast majority of people will become true Revolutionaries.

We will know that we are being successful, raising the level of awareness of the working class, when the marches and demonstrations carry banners and posters which read:

Workers of the World, Unite!

Dictatorship of the Proletariat!

Soviet Power1

World Socialist Republic!

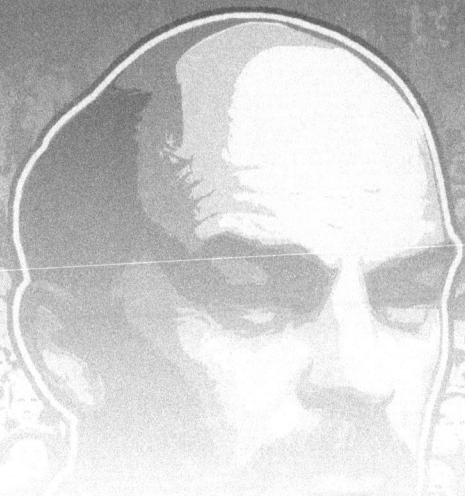

# CHAPTER 6

## Presidential Election of 2024

Now that the midterm elections are over, the presidential election campaigning of 2024 has already begun, even though not all of the midterm ballots have been counted. The American people cannot get a break from all the political posturing!

Yet all of this campaigning for an election, which is still two years away, reveals the entire range of thinking of the class of people who are running the country. Of course, I am referring to the billionaires, technically referred to as the bourgeoisie. More accurately, it reveals their mind boggling stupidity!

Even the billionaires are now admitting that they are at a crisis point, with a "severe recession imminent", high inflation, crime "out of control", immigration plagued by an "open border", and widespread "voter discontent". This does not stop them from resorting to "verbal gymnastics", in an effort to avoid using the word capitalism. Instead, they use the word "democracy".

Their most visible "headache" comes in the form of one of their own, Donald Trump by name, a former president, a member of their class, a successful capitalist, a fellow billionaire. That boy just will not "play by the rules"!

The rules are that government officials must lie and deceive. The working people, the class of people they crush and exploit, must be "kept in the dark". Under no circumstances must working people be told the truth! Yet Trump once again "shot his mouth off", and blurted out that which everyone knew, but was supposed to deny! These are his very words:

"The citizens of our country have not yet realized the full extent and gravity of the pain our nation is going through, and the total effect of the suffering is just starting to take hold," Trump said. "They don't quite feel it yet, but they will very soon. I have no doubt that by 2024 it will sadly be much worse, and they will see much more clearly what happened and what is happening to our country. And the voting will be much different. Twenty twenty-four. Are you getting ready? And I am too. I am too."

In fact, Trump is correct when he states that "by 2024 it will sadly be much worse", *unless the working people take action!* Of course, I am referring to the working class, the proletariat, as well as the lower strata of the middle class, the petty bourgeois.

As a monopoly capitalist, an imperialist, Trump is well aware of the fact that capitalism gives rise to periodic crises. In this, he is correct.

As Lenin stated, in Imperialism, the Highest Stage of Capitalism: "Crises of every kind -economic crises more frequently, but not only these- in their turn increase very considerably the tendency towards concentration and monopoly". Today we are facing an economic crisis, along with a political crisis.

It was Marx and Engels who explained these crises, in The Communist Manifesto:

"A similar movement is going on before our own eyes. Modern bourgeois society, with its relations of production, of exchange and of property, a society that has conjured up such gigantic means of production and of exchange, is like the sorcerer who is no longer able to control the powers of the nether world whom he has called up by his spells. For many a decade past the history of industry and commerce is but the history of the revolt of modern productive forces against modern conditions of production, against the property relations that are the conditions for the existence of the bourgeois and of its rule. It is enough to mention the commercial crises that by their periodical return put the existence of the entire bourgeois society on its trial, each time more threateningly. In these crises, a great part not only of the existing products, but also of the previously created productive forces, are periodically destroyed. In these crises, there breaks out an epidemic that, in all earlier epochs, would have seemed an absurdity — the epidemic of over-production. Society suddenly finds itself put back into a state of momentary barbarism; it appears as if a famine, a universal war of devastation, had cut off the supply of every means of subsistence; industry and commerce seem to be destroyed; and why? Because there is too much civilization, too much means of subsistence, too much industry, too much commerce. The productive forces at the disposal of society no longer tend to further the development of the conditions of bourgeois property; on the contrary, they have become too powerful for these conditions, by which they are fettered, and so soon as they overcome these fetters, they bring disorder into the whole of bourgeois society, endanger the existence of bourgeois property. The conditions of bourgeois society are too narrow to comprise the wealth created by them. And how does the bourgeoisie get over these crises? On the one hand by enforced destruction of a mass of productive forces; on the other, by the conquest of new markets, and by the more thorough exploitation of the old ones. That is to say, by paving the way for more extensive and more destructive crises, and by diminishing the means whereby crises are prevented.

"The weapons with which the bourgeoisie felled feudalism to the ground are now used against the bourgeoisie."

That is precisely the current state of affairs! We have here a crisis in capitalism, in no small part because we *have too much!* So many people are hungry, homeless, unemployed or under employed, because of over production! Because we have a *vast surplus!* Truly, that which was considered to be an "absurdity", in years gone by, is now a reality!

Naturally, as a typical capitalist, Trump embraces this "absurdity". He is well aware that the "destruction of a mass of productive forces" is currently taking place. Of course that will in turn lead to further mass unemployment, countless more workers out of work, hungry, cold and homeless, but that is of no consequence to the capitalists.

The Communist Manifesto also mentions the workers, the proletarians, those whom the capitalists "discard", much as we throw away old newspapers:

"But not only has the bourgeoisie forged the weapons that bring death to itself; it has also called into existence the men who will wield those weapons - the modern working class - the proletarians."

No member of the capitalist class, the bourgeoisie, including Trump, can imagine the proletariat, the working class, rising up in revolt. Hence the reason that Trump, as well as other billionaires, are openly predicting that "things are bound to get much worse".

This crisis in capitalism has spread across the country. In particular, the governor of the state of Texas has effectively announced that he plans to *go to war with the "army of invading immigrants"!*

No doubt, many people are thinking that the governor was merely posturing, making threats which he absolutely did not plan to implement. America could not possibly go to war with defenceless civilians! Think again! Recently, border officials separated mothers from their young children, and then locked up those children in jails! That is quite possibly still happening! It stands to reason that the people responsible for such actions, are also capable of mass murder!

The Governor of Texas has "justified" this proposed war on unarmed civilians, including women and children, by invoking a clause of the American Constitution. That clause, Article 1, Section 10, is as follows:

*"No State shall, without the Consent of Congress, lay any Duty of Tonnage, keep Troops, or Ships of War in time of Peace, enter into any Agreement or Compact with another State, or with a foreign Power, or engage in War, unless actually invaded, or in such imminent Danger as will not admit of delay.*

This article I downloaded from the Internet, hence the italics.

The governor of Texas is arguing that unarmed civilians, families who are attempting to escape poverty, persecution and violence, amount to an *invading army*!

It is significant that Trump agrees with that Governor. It is also significant that the act of an individual state, "going to war", would almost certainly result in that state *separating from the Union!*

Texas was, at one time, a self declared separate country, and will very likely, once again, become a separate republic. The American Empire just moved one step closer to dissolution.

In this article, I have focused upon Donald Trump and the Republican Party. There is a reason for this. They are in the news! That is the only reason I have focused upon them! The Democratic Party is also in disarray! Both Parties serve the same class! As that is the case, the two are equally reactionary! They are part of the same state apparatus, which has to be destroyed, at the time of the Revolution!

The current situation is absolutely Revolutionary! Various "crises in capitalism" have come together, at the same time, and created the "perfect storm"! The capitalists are "at their wits end"! They do not know "which way to jump"! Which is not to say that the system is going to collapse, under its own weight! It is not going to collapse! It has to be destroyed! That can only happen through Revolution!

This is to stress the fact that a Revolution can be successful, only if it follows the Revolutionary guidelines of Marx and Lenin. This is to say that the existing state apparatus, which has been set up by the capitalists, in order to crush the working class, must be destroyed. It must be replaced by a different state apparatus, in order to crush the capitalists, as they try to "restore their paradise lost". That state apparatus is referred to as the Dictatorship of the Proletariat. It is to be administered through the medium of the Soviets.

For the members of the working class who have just recently become politically active, or "woke up", I can urge you to read State and Revolution, by Lenin. He wrote that article immediately before the Great October Socialist Russian Revolution. That Revolution was successful, but only because the Revolutionaries followed the Revolutionary line, laid down by Lenin.

Perhaps a word of caution is in order. You can expect the "social chauvinists" to oppose the "smashing of the existing state apparatus". There is a good reason for their opposition. Their plan is to "take over" the existing state apparatus, at the time of the Revolution, and set themselves up, as the new rulers. Perish forbid! They too, are in the service of the capitalists! Their choice! They must be treated accordingly.

As most people enjoy company, may I suggest that workers get together on the Internet, through computer programs of some sort, and discuss the Revolutionary works of Marx and Lenin. It may help to think of it as a book club, as that is precisely the case. At the same time, you can form Councils, otherwise known as Soviets, and prepare for Revolution. I have covered this in a separate article, so there is no need to go into detail here.

Bear in mind that Revolution is "right around the corner". The success of that Revolution depends upon the most advanced members of the Proletariat. As you are reading this article, that very likely means you!

We will know that the Revolution is sure to be successful, when certain expressions become common place:

Workers of the World, Unite!

Dictatorship of the Proletariat!

Soviet Power!

World Socialist Republic!

# CHAPTER 7

## The Absurdity of
## Inclusive Capitalism

The revolutionary motion that is sweeping North America is very powerful. In fact, it has spread to the industrialize countries of the world. The capitalists are clearly "feeling the heat", are unable to rule in the old way, so that they are being forced to change their method of rule. Their latest brain storm is to "preach the gospel" of a "strengthened democracy", which is that of a "new and improved", "Inclusive Capitalism".

This program is being spearheaded by the Obama Foundation. The mission of that Foundation is to "inspire, empower and connect people to change their world". Clearly, the wording of that mission statement was carefully chosen, as it does not specify just *how* it plans to inspire, *which* people with whom to connect, and just *how* to change the world. This is to say that it is devoid of class content. Yet it very likely attracts some very well meaning people, mainly young ones, especially those who are determined to "make a difference".

The Foundation has a Leaders Program, which has the goal "to inspire, empower and connect regional cohorts of change makers to accelerate positive and lasting change in their communities and throughout the world." This too is carefully worded, also devoid of class content.

The Foundation has other Programs, including a Girls Opportunity Unity Alliance, a Voyager Scholarship, a Fellowship Program and a Scholars Program. No doubt a great many dedicated young people are drawn to this Foundation. In this article, I will focus on their latest program, the Democracy Forum.

About a week ago, Michelle Obama launched the Democracy Forum. Her speech is on the Internet, lasts around a minute, and her delivery was impeccable. The people who coached her, referred to as her "handlers", did a fine job! Every detail was carefully orchestrated! The clothes were selected, as was her hair style. Her tone of voice was one of concern, as was her facial expression, not to mention her body language. That in no way changes the fact that her speech was pure Hog Wash!

Yet this speech is vitally important, as it is a clear cut example of the change in the method of rule, adopted by the capitalists, the billionaires, the bourgeoisie. For that reason, I have chosen to give the full speech:

"Democracy: It's more than a system of government. It's a set of values. Freedom. Justice. Equality. Openness. Truth. It's not about blood or pedigree or wealth. It's about making sure everyone has a voice and a fair shot. And it's up to all of us, as individuals, to not only hope for a better future, but work together to build one. So we have got to push each other, and lean on one another, and recognize the power each one of us has, to ensure that this moment is not a twilight, but a dawning of the next great chapter of democracy around the world. And that is exactly what we are here to do."

Dear lady, you are so right, when you say that "Democracy" is "more than a system of government". Democracy is a *method of class rule!* It involves a state apparatus! It is the police, prisons, courts, bureaucracy and standing army, which is used to suppress the working class! It is a method, by which one *class* of people, in our case the capitalists, the billionaires, the bourgeoisie, use to crush and exploit the members of another *class*, in our case the working class, the wage labourers, the proletariat.

It has nothing to do with a "set of values". It has everything to do with *"power and wealth"!* The billionaires are concerned with one thing, and one thing only, their *profit,* their *bottom line!* The billionaires are *focused!* The billionaires are *determined!* They are *focused* and *determined* to become *Trillionaires!* That has nothing to do with "voice" and "fair shot" of "everyone", which is to say the working class!

You are also correct when you say that "it's up to all of us", to "work together" to "build a better future". At least, it is correct if you are referring to the members of the working class! That can only happen under *socialism!*

The only "better future", is a future without capitalism! A future of Socialism. A future in which people will be working together, for the common good. A future that is possible *only* under S*ocialism!*

Under capitalism, we have "democracy", but *democracy for the capitalists!* For the proletariat, we live under a *dictatorship!* The dictatorship of the bourgeoisie!

Lenin explains, quite clearly, in State and Revolution, that your "democracy" consists of a "state apparatus", a "special repressive force" for the "suppression of the proletariat by the bourgeoisie, for the suppression of the millions of toilers by the handful of rich", which is to say the capitalists, the billionaires. He goes on to say that this state apparatus must be smashed, at the time of the Revolution, and replaced by a "special repressive force" for the suppression of the capitalists, the billionaires, by the working class. This is referred to as the Dictatorship of the Proletariat.

Yet the Obama Foundation has set up a Forum, one with ambitious goals. The spokesman for that Forum is the former Chairman of the Council of Economic Advisers. As such, he is, without doubt, a dedicated supporter of capitalism. He also has a two minute speech on the Internet, titled Obama Foundation Democracy Forum. This too, I found to be most interesting. It may help to think of this as their "new and improved" proposed method of rule:

"If you want to strengthen democracy, you also have to think about the economy. And what does that mean? I would highlight three things:

"The first is, from an economic perspective, there is a serious question of whether growth is more sustainable and stable when everyone benefits, versus when only a very few benefit. You see around the world and in the United States, special interests, changing the tax code, changing regulations, to benefit a small group of people that undermines and accentuates the ordinary people that they cannot get ahead, and they can't win.

"The second thing is that we have seen over recent decades that as there are big increases in economic inequality, there are also big increases in social polarization and in the efforts of the few and the special interests to make sure they get theirs, and that our politics gets biased towards those with money. That leads to number three.

"The rise of distrust in our institutions, the rise of cynicism among voters and citizens. They no longer trust that the government is looking out for them. That is why it is so important for democracy that we make sure that it is an inclusive capitalism and inclusive growth.

"At the Obama Foundation Democracy Forum, we are bringing in leaders that are proposing approaches and solutions that are responsive to citizens and create inclusive and equitable economic realities for everyone."

It is quite surprising to find that this man has stated the facts, quite accurately, while at the same time, carefully avoiding class terms. His reference to the "few", the "very few", "small group of people", and "those with money", is a reference to the capitalists, the billionaires, the bourgeoisie. His reference to "everyone", "ordinary people", to "voters and citizens", is a reference to the common people, the working class, the members of the public, the proletariat.

He starts out by making the point that "growth is more sustainable and stable when everyone benefits", as opposed to our current situation, "when only a few benefit". This is a result of "changing the tax code" and "changing regulations", so that the capitalists, the billionaires pay little taxes, if any at all. It is the working class, the "ordinary people", that pays all the taxes! Those same "ordinary people" are well aware of this, aware that we "cannot get ahead", that we "cannot win"! But only because we live under capitalism!

In his second "highlight", he points to the "economic inequality", which has led to "social polarization", as the capitalists make sure they "get theirs", as the government policies are "biased towards those with money". This is a convoluted way of saying that which everyone knows, the "rich are getting richer", while the "poor are getting poorer"! The poor, the working people, are also well aware of the fact that the government makes sure that the rich get ever more rich!

His third "highlight" also says that working people are now cynical! Not at all! Workers merely see now that the government is "looking out for" the capitalists! Of course they no longer trust the government! That is not cynical! That is merely facing the facts!

He deserves credit for stating certain facts, even though in a convoluted manner, while carefully avoiding any mention of the existence of classes. He even went so far as to acknowledge the fact that the working class no longer trusts the government. His proposed solution to this problem is to make *capitalism inclusive!*

This *cannot be done!* Capitalism is anything but inclusive! Perhaps someone should explain to this simple soul- the former Chairman of the Council of Economic Advisors!- the "nuts and bolts" of capitalism!

The capitalists own the "means of production", which is to say the factories, mills, mines, the land and buildings, as well as everything else that is used to produce goods. They also own all of the "means of transportation", which is to say railroads, airlines, shipping lines and trucking companies, for example. They also own all communications networks, such as the Internet, radio and television stations, newspapers and so forth. In fact, they own anything and everything of any considerable value. They regard this property as "capital", as indeed it is. Their one and only income is from their "invested capital". That is the reason they are referred to as "capitalists".

They do no useful work. They merely collect interest on that invested capital. They contribute nothing to society! They are leaches! Human parasites!

These capitalists, those who are commonly referred to as billionaires, are part of a separate class, technically referred to as the bourgeoisie. They are small in number, but very powerful, because of their great wealth.

As opposed to the class of capitalists, we have the working class, technically referred to as the proletariat. As we have no "capital", we are forced to sell our labour power. We work for the capitalists, if only because we have no choice in the matter. We sell ourselves by the hour, so that we are "wage slaves".

It is in the interests of the workers, the proletarians, to sell ourselves at the highest possible price, while it is in the interests of the capitalists, the bourgeois, to pay us as little as possible. It does not take a "rocket scientist" to figure out that our interests are "diametrically opposed"! That which is in the best interests of the workers, is in the worst interests of the capitalists!

We are class enemies! There is a constant state of war going on between workers and capitalists, proletarians and bourgeoisie! Usually this war is hidden, but occasionally it breaks out into the open. When this happens, it is referred to as Revolution! We are close to open Revolution, as capitalism has reached the point of crisis, and the capitalists are forced to change their method of rule. Hence the nonsense of "inclusive capitalism"!

It was Lenin who gave a very clear definition of democracy, in State and Revolution. In referring to the democratic republic, under capitalism: "Democracy for an insignificant minority, democracy for the rich - that is the democracy of capitalist society." This is to drive home the fact that democracy, under capitalism, *cannot be inclusive!* It is strictly for the "insignificant minority"!

Yet we cannot help but feeling grateful to the Obama Foundation, and especially to the Democracy Forum, for drawing the attention of so many members of the working class, to the issue of democracy. We can only hope that they will continue to point out the hypocrisy of democracy under capitalism, bourgeois democracy.

This will no doubt inspire working people to read State and Revolution. In this way, we will all be more prepared for the forth coming Revolution. I can think of no better way to close this article than with my usual slogans. I can only hope that these will soon become common place expressions:

Workers of the World, Unite!

Soviet Power!

Dictatorship of the Proletariat!

World Socialist Republic!

# CHAPTER 8

## Eve of Revolution

The press is now reporting that the railroads may soon shut down. As they phrased it, "On the eve of the holiday season, workers at the heart of the supply chain are once again threatening to strike". They report that if no deal is reached by December 8, or even as early as December 5, "the railroads could lock workers out, or the workers could go on strike".

There are a number of unions involved, but if even one of them goes on strike, none of the other unions will cross the picket lines. This would immediately bring to a halt the freight that is moved by rail in the country, roughly thirty percent of the total. It would also effect some Amtrak and commuter rail systems, as they operate on tracks that are owned by the freight railroads.

It is clear that the press is biased towards the owners of the railroads, as their main concern is with the "disastrous 2 billion dollar a day hit to our economy". With that in mind, they quite cheerfully report that, "Should there be a strike,

Congress would likely intervene within hours. The Railway Labour Act allows Congress to take any number of measures to get trains running again - including imposing some version of the contract or extending the status quo, kicking any decision to the next Congress".

In this, the journalists are supremely optimistic. Just because Congress has the authority to act, does not mean that they are prepared to do so. It is far more likely that Congress will do that which it does best, which is "pass the buck", or as the press reports, "kicking any decision to the next Congress", which convenes on January 3. Or at least, they may try! Even if Congress "legislates the railroad workers" back to work, that does not mean that the workers will return to work!

Some of the most highly respected politicians, from both mainstream Parties, Republican and Democratic, are predicting "widespread chaos" in both Houses of Congress. That is perhaps the kindest forecast. The more cynical ones are comparing it to "the lunatics taking over the asylum". No one can deny that both Parties are deeply divided. Many within the Democratic Party want to git rid of President Biden, while many Republicans want to get rid of Trump. Yet neither leader is prepared to "relinquish the reins of power", and each has a sizeable following within his Party.

The Democrats have a "razor thin" majority in the Senate, with a couple Senators considered to be "loose cannons". This is to say that they have a rather annoying habit of "thinking for themselves", not always voting along Party lines.

By contrast, it is the Republicans who have a "razor thin" majority in the House, but they too have Members who are also considered to be unreliable. The point is that neither Party has any great confidence of passing, or blocking, any piece of legislation.

It is clear that the working class, including the members of Unions, are completely fed up. Apparently the railroad workers have been trying to negotiate a contract for three years. It was only after President Biden "intervened" and appointed an "Emergency Board", that the Union leaders were able to sit down with the railroad owners, and a "Framework" agreement was reached. This contract was rejected by the Union members, the rank and file. The proposed raise in wages barely covers the cost of living increase. As well, the main "sticking point" is the "quality of life" issues, which were not resolved.

Yet the journalists, although biased, were correct in stating the fact that "other workers are making their voices heard". These workers include the nurses, mental health workers, warehouse workers who are trying to form unions, and others. Although the journalists did not mention the "others" by name, the fact is that they include the truckers!

In fact, it was the truckers who took part in the Freedom Convoy! It was the truckers who occupied downtown Ottawa! It was the truckers who shut down the Ambassador Bridge! It was the truckers who closed various other border crossings! It was the truckers who were joined by numerous farmers! It was the truckers protest, including the Freedom Convoy, that - temporarily! - became side tracked.

The issues the truckers protested against, have not been resolved! On the contrary, they have intensified! The truckers have not lost interest! It is quite possible - even likely!- that any railroad strike will be joined by those who haul the other seventy percent of the freight in the country! The truckers!

The history of previous Revolutions have shown that such uprisings usually start in the transportation industry. This is to say that it is usually the railroad workers that first go on strike. After the trains quit running, the workers in other industries join them. With industry shut down, workers take to the streets, frequently storm the prisons and release the inmates, and attack the houses and businesses of their class enemies, in our case the capitalists. Given the proper leadership, they also overthrow the government, smash the existing state apparatus, and set up a new workers government, under the new state apparatus, called the Dictatorship of the Proletariat.

At least, that is precisely the thing that happened in October of 1917, in Russia. It has since gone down in history as the Great October Socialist Revolution. It was successful because, at that time, the country was blessed with a true Communist Party, led by Lenin.

I stress this because it is so important. It is quite possible, if not likely, that the Revolution will break out very soon. I say this because the fact of the matter is that Soviets, or Councils, first appeared during the Russian Revolution of 1905. They were then crushed at the time the Revolution was crushed, in 1907. Yet they spontaneously reappeared in the build up to the February Revolution of 1917. The point is that Soviets appear during, or immediately before, a Revolution. In fact, Soviets have already appeared in America! It means that the American Revolution is very close!

Yet as Lenin pointed out, in What Is To Be Done?, "Without a Revolutionary theory, there can be no Revolutionary movement".

As for those who doubt that previous statement, bear in mind that at the beginning of the twentieth century, there were no less than three Revolutions in Russia. The first two were completely spontaneous, as all the Marxists at that time, those who were first referred to as Social Democrats and later as Bolsheviks, had been thrown in jail and were either killed or exiled. Lenin had been exiled.

The first Revolution, that of 1905, raged for two years, and was then crushed. Although it failed to achieve its stated goals, it managed to dispel any illusions the common people had, concerning the Czar and the government. It also succeeded in training a great many workers and peasants, in preparation for the second Russian Revolution of the twentieth century, that of February, 1917. That second Russian Revolution succeeded in overthrowing the Czar, so that a democratic republic was established.

That was as far as the working people could go! They could go no farther! Without the proper leaders, Socialism was out of the question!

Under that democratic republic, the slaughter of the First World War continued. The common people were cold and hungry. Inflation sky rocketed, so that basic necessities were out of reach. Crime was out of control, so that people dared not step out of their homes. Sound familiar?

The Russian Revolution is so important, as it so closely resembles our own. The situation is so similar. The people who took part in the Occupy Movement, of twenty year ago, also had their illusions dispelled. They learned that the government does not represent them. They also learned some valuable lessons in the class struggle. They are now veterans, just as those who took part in the earlier anti war movement, are also veterans.

As is well known, Lenin was able to return to Russia in April of 1917. Of course the capitalists had to be overthrown, and with that in mind, he wrote State and Revolution. It may help to think of that as a "road map", a "detailed guide" to overthrowing the capitalists and establishing a Socialist society, as that is precisely the case. An understanding of that Revolutionary book is essential to conducting a successful Socialist Revolution.

That book is required reading for all Revolutionaries. Lenin makes the point that the existing state apparatus, which has been set up by the capitalists, in our case the billionaires, the bourgeoisie, with the express purpose of crushing the working people, the proletariat, must be *smashed!* It must in turn be replaced by a new state apparatus, in the form of the Dictatorship of the Proletariat.

The reason for this is that after the Revolution, the capitalists will be determined to regain their "paradise lost"! They will stoop to any level, any bit of deception, to achieve this goal. Hence the need to crush their resistance. That Dictatorship of the Proletariat will be administered through the Soviets. In English, these Soviets are referred to as Councils.

The importance of smashing the existing state apparatus must be stressed. Otherwise the social chauvinists, those who are merely Socialists in words, chauvinists in deeds, will attempt to take over this apparatus, at the time of the Revolution, and use it for their own purposes. This is to say that they will set themselves up as the new rulers. That is the last thing we need!

There is a sense of urgency in this matter, that of preparing for the approaching Revolution. The situation is certainly Revolutionary. Lenin goes into this, in detail, in Left Wing Communism, An Infantile Disorder. As he put it, "It is only when the *'lower classes' do not want* to live in the old way and the 'upper classes' *cannot carry on in the old way* that the Revolution can triumph". (italics by Lenin)

That is precisely the situation we have now. Among the "lower classes", we have the wage labourers, those who are paid by the hour, the proletariat. As well, there are the family farmers, those who are referred to as peasants, in most parts of the world. Then there are the small business owners, the lower strata of the middle class, the petty bourgeois. These include those who own machines, such as trucks, and work for themselves. Collectively, these are the "lower classes" of people who refuse to continue to live in the "old way".

As for the "upper classes", which is to say the monopoly capitalists, the billionaires, the bourgeoisie, it is clear that they "cannot carry on in the old way". They are squabbling among themselves. In fact, it is safe to say that "they are at each other's throats"!

Both Houses of Congress are practically dead locked, or soon will be. The country is about to "hit the debt ceiling" on December 15, and could shut down, unless the Congress takes action, once again raising the debt ceiling. As the capitalists are fighting among themselves, this is unlikely. The whole country could be facing bankruptcy. The trains could quit running as early as December 5, and the truckers could join them. Other unions could also join them. In fact, the whole country could shut down! That is the very definition of Revolution!

Yet without the leaders who are aware of the Revolutionary theories of Marx and Lenin, and prepared to put those theories into action, nothing of substance will change! We will remain under capitalism! No Scientific Socialism!

There is a difference between modern day America - and not just America! - and Russia, in 1917. At that time, in Russia, a Communist Party was in place. The members of the Party were able to explain to people the basic tenets of

Marxism. Such is no longer the case! The Communist Party no longer exists in America.

The members of the Russian Communist Party led the Revolution to victory. We do not have an American Communist Party, so in a sense, our task is more difficult. Yet as no Revolution is "made to order", it will happen when it happens. As that is the case, we are going to have to prepare for the Revolution, and at the same time form a true Communist Party, one which calls for Soviet Power and the Dictatorship of the Proletariat. There is *no other way!*

Then again, this may not be quite as difficult as it appears, on first glance. Most common people are literate, own computers and know how to use them. Those who are more advanced can be expected to download Revolutionary literature. As well, Revolutionary books by Marx and Lenin can be ordered, through the Internet. A careful reading of those key works can go a long way towards raising their level of awareness, to that of true Revolutionaries.

It is also a fact that as the Revolution gains strength, we can expect ever more people to become swept up into the whirlwind of Revolution. It is reasonable to expect that those who were "hitherto apathetic", even among the intellectual members of the middle class, will become politically active. Many of these people are well aware of the Revolutionary theories of Marx and Lenin. We can expect those people to help create a proper Communist Parry.

There are also the veterans of the Occupy Movement of the previous generation. They can testify to the fact that without a Revolutionary theory, there can be no Revolutionary movement. They speak from experience! Bitter experience! They tried! They made a supreme effort! The result was nil! No doubt they have been tempered in the struggle. Now they are veterans! The same is true of the older generation, those who have the experience of the anti war movement.

The people who took part in the Womens' March, of recent memory, can also be expected to rise up, once again. That was supremely well organized! We can use such people in our movement! Ladies, feel free to broaden your horizons! Become more ambitious! No need to be shy! Place no restrictions on yourself! Experience has proven to you that there is no point in fighting for paltry reforms! Half measures get you nowhere! Revolution! Overthrow the capitalists! Show the world how to "fight like a girl"! Scientific Socialism! Soviet Power and Dictatorship of the Proletariat!

Currently the common people, by whom I mean the working class, the proletariat, as well as the lower strata of the middle class, the petty bourgeois, are doing their best. As they read the most essential Revolutionary works, that of Marx and Lenin, their level of awareness will rise. Yet they could use the help of middle class intellectuals.

It is in the best interest of intellectuals to play a vital role in the Revolution. After the Revolution, their services will be in demand, and they can expect to be rewarded, paid quite handsomely. Besides, those who are taking part in the Revolution, will have no fear of becoming a target of that Revolution. The same cannot be said of the intellectuals who oppose the Revolution!

Perhaps a word of caution is in order: Be discreet! Do not make it easy for the various governmental police agencies! There is no need to meet in person! Use the Internet! Make it clear that Soviet Power, and the Dictatorship of the Proletariat, is at the heart of the program of the Party! Those of us who support those two fundamental goals, can put aside any other differences we may have, and work together. Those who are opposed to either one, are not eligible for membership.

Be active in Soviets, or Councils, if that is the name you prefer. As I have documented in other writings, that is the best way to prepare for the Revolution, and especially the Insurrection. There is no need to repeat it here.

Bear in mind that the Soviets appeared spontaneously, in Russia, at the time of the Revolution. Within a short time, they were so powerful, they rivalled the power of the Provisional Government. These Soviets are not to be underestimated! They have recently made an appearance in America. Do not be surprised if they soon challenge the authority of the government! The Second American Revolution is imminent!

We will know that the Revolution is going to be successful, that the capitalists, the billionaires, are about to be overthrown, when the protesters carry signs and posters which proclaim:

Soviet Power!

Dictatorship of the Proletariat!

Workers of the World, Unite!

World Socialist Republic!

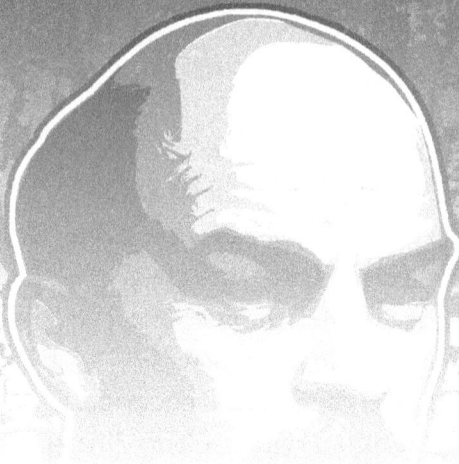

# CHAPTER 9

......................................................................................................................

## World Socialist Revolution

The first Russian Revolution of the twentieth century, referred to as the Revolution of 1905, or simply Oh Five, began on January 22, old style calendar, OSC, or January 9, new style calendar, NSC, of that year. At that time, in the capital city of Saint Petersburg, a priest, by the name of Father Gapon, led a procession of unarmed citizens to the Winter Palace of Czar Nicholas of Russia. As the loyal subjects of His Majesty, their one and only desire was to present to their monarch a petition, with a list of their legitimate grievances. In response, Czar Nicholas turned loose his Imperial Guard. By the end of the day, the streets of Saint Petersburg were littered with the bodies of countless dead and wounded Russian citizens.

This has gone down in Russian history as "Bloody Sunday".

Incidentally, at that time, they were using the Old Style Calendar, OSC, as opposed to the New Style Calendar,

NSC. For the purposes of this article, I use the abbreviation of OSC and NSC.

Historians consider Bloody Sunday to be the start of the Revolution of 1905. As outrage spread across the country, a series of massive strikes spread across the industrial centres of the Russian Empire. The trains quit running. In outlying areas, the peasants attacked the landlords. Prisons were stormed and the inmates were released. For two years, the Russian Empire was shaken, but it did not collapse. In 1907, the uprising died down, and Czar Nicholas was still in power. There followed several years of reaction.

Not all Revolutions can be assigned a start date.

The European Revolution of 1848 is one such Revolution. Historians are agreed that it started in Sicily, in January of 1848, and spread across much of Europe. These are referred to as "republic revolts", in that the citizens rose up against their monarchies. All ended in failure, followed by widespread reaction, as the various monarchs punished the common people, for the terrible sin of challenging their "betters", daring to demand democratic rights.

It is significant that this Revolution has characteristics which are common to all modern Revolutions. They tend to spread! Even though it started in Sicily, it did not end there! The industrial Revolution has given rise to communications networks, which were completely unknown to our ancestors. We are now at the point of being made aware of events taking place, around the world, as they happen!

To return to Russia of the early twentieth century, after the Revolution of "Oh Five", reaction set in, as it always does, after the suppression of a mass movement. For several years, things "returned to normal", in the sense that the trains were running, the factories were producing, the peasants were growing their crops, the nobility was living a life of luxury, and the capitalists were making nothing but money! Life was good! At least for the "upper classes"! They thought nothing had changed! They could not possibly have been more mistaken! The situation had changed, and changed quite dramatically! They just did not know it!

At the start of the Oh Five Revolution, the "common people", by whom I mean the workers and peasants, were the loyal subjects of His Majesty. After the Revolution, they remained the subjects of His Majesty. Just not so loyal.

That Revolution had succeeded in revealing, to common people, the true nature of the nobility! They were concerned only with their power and wealth! Any challenge to their authority was simply not allowed! Their response to the legitimate demands of the common people of Russia, left no room for any doubt!

In scientific jargon, we can say that the "level of awareness" of the masses had been raised. (I tend to generally avoid the use of the word "masses", in reference to people, as it sounds so impersonal. I prefer the expression "common people", or "working people", or the "rank and file", as that is the manner in which they refer to themselves.)

It is also a fact that they were veterans! There is no substitute for experience! Those who took part in the Oh Five Revolution, knew what to expect! What is more, they knew how to respond!

As is well known, after several years of reaction, the Revolutionary motion picked up again. Only this time, it was much stronger! The common people had no illusions! They recognized the Czar as the butcher that he was! Nicholas the Bloody! They were focused on removing him from power, and they did! In February of 1917, he was overthrown. Not that the bourgeois writers state it in those terms. Those writers say that the Czar was forced to "abdicate the throne".

For that reason, the second Russian Revolution of the twentieth century became known as the February Revolution. It is one of those Revolutions which has not been given a "start date". This is understandable, as a Revolution comes about as the result of a mass movement. Yet some mass movements give rise to Revolutions, while others do not. Frequently, there is no clear distinction between the two. It generally comes down to common usage. As I am not terribly concerned with titles, I consider this to be a matter of indifference.

One such mass movement, of recent times, is that of the Occupy Movement. At no point has anyone referred to it as a Revolution. Be that as it may, it has been assigned a "start date" of September 17, 2011. On that day, a group of people occupied a park in New York City. The bourgeois press referred to this as the "'beginning of a populist socio-politico movement".

It is important to remember that the "press" is completely owned and operated by the capitalists, the billionaires, the bourgeoisie. Those who work for them, referred to as journalists, are careful to report events precisely in a manner of which the capitalists approve. These journalists are referred to as "bourgeois", as they are loyal, devoted servants of their "lords and masters", the bourgeoisie. For that reason, it is important to "read between the lines", to distinguish between the *facts* they state, as opposed to their analysis.

The following report is an example:

"The first Occupy protest to receive widespread attention, <u>Occupy Wall Street</u> in <u>Zuccotti Park</u>, <u>Lower Manhattan</u>, began on 17 September 2011. By 9 October, Occupy protests had taken place or were ongoing in <u>over 951</u>

cities across 82 countries, and in over 600 communities in the United States. Although the movement became most active in the United States, by October 2011 Occupy protests and occupations had started in dozens of other countries across every widely inhabited continent. For the first month, overt police repression remained minimal, but this began to change by 25 October 2011, when police first attempted to forcibly remove Occupy Oakland. By the end of 2011 authorities had cleared most of the major camps, with the last remaining high-profile sites – in Washington, D.C. and in London – evicted by February 2012."

This paragraph is somewhat exceptional, in the sense that it is rather accurate. It merely states the facts, without giving any analysis. The fact is that the Occupy Movement, was a *Revolutionary Movement,* one which started and spread *around the world* within a matter of *days!*

When I say "around the world", I am referring mainly to the countries of the world which are industrialized. Sometimes I over simplify, in order to make a point.

The writer is also correct in documenting the fact that the various government agencies wasted no time in crushing that Revolutionary Movement. In that process, the democratic rights of all citizens, in all capitalist countries, to peaceful protest, was disregarded. In each country, the class of people in charge, the capitalists, the billionaires, the bourgeoisie, made it abundantly clear, that they will tolerate no challenge to their authority.

In the following paragraph, the writer "reverted to form" and presented more facts, but complete with a "proper analysis", in the sense that it was biased, or "slanted", in favour of the capitalists:

"The Occupy movement took inspiration in part from the Arab Spring, from the 2009 Iranian Green Movement, and from the Spanish Indignados Movement, as well as from the overall global wave of anti-austerity protests of 2010 and following. The movement commonly used the slogan "We are the 99%" and the #Occupy hashtag format; it organized through websites such as the now defunct Occupy Together. According to *The Washington Post*, the movement, which Cornel West described as a "democratic awakening", is difficult to distill to a few demands. On 12 October 2011, the Los Angeles City Council became one of the first governmental bodies in the United States to adopt a resolution stating its informal support of the Occupy movement. In October 2012, the Executive Director of Financial Stability at the Bank of England stated that the protesters were right to criticise and had persuaded bankers and politicians "to behave in a more moral way".

It is true that the protesters referred to themselves as the "99%", as opposed to the "1%". This is a step towards class consciousness, or perhaps it is more accurate to say that it is "class consciousness in embryonic form". There was an "instinctive awareness" on the part of the "vast majority", or the "common people", or the "rank and file", as they refer to themselves. They instinctively distinguished themselves, the 99%, from the "insignificant minority", the "extremely rich", whom they referred to as the 1%.

All of those protesters were either working class, proletarians, or middle class, petty bourgeois. This calls for a little explanation, which some readers may find to be tiresome. Yet it is important, so bear with me.

Working class people are composed of those who have nothing to sell but their labour power. They sell themselves by the hour, for the fine reason that they have no choice in the matter. It is either that or starvation. Yet the conditions of life of the working class do not lead to the awareness of themselves as a class. The scientific name for this class is that of "proletariat".

The middle class people are those who may own a small business. They have something to sell. They are "small time capitalists", or "petty bourgeois". They are under extreme pressure from the monopoly corporations, as those who own those corporations, the billionaires, or "bourgeoisie", take a "dim view" of competition. In fact, they are determined to wipe out all competition, no matter how minor.

In short, these are the three main classes of people in North America. The bourgeoisie, the proletariat, and the petty bourgeois. The middle class has been decimated, but is still a force. The class of peasants, or farmers, have been all but wiped out. They are "hanging on by their finger tips".

In other parts of the world, the peasants are still quite numerous. In certain countries, they make up the majority of the population. The Revolutionaries, in such countries, must take this into account.

The point being that during the Occupy Movement, the class of people known as the proletariat, as well as the class of people known as the petty bourgeois, came together and demanded change. The class of people known as the bourgeoisie, those who are in charge, made it quite clear that they will tolerate no discontent.

Now to return to the second paragraph. Perhaps the most glaring absurdity is the statement that "the protesters... had persuaded the bankers and politicians to 'behave in a more moral way'". *Nonsense!* The "bankers and politicians", to whom the writer of this article refers, are the loyal and devoted servants of the the capitalists, the billionaires, the bourgeoisie! Such people are not capable of acting "in a moral way"! They are strangers to morality! They would not know a moral, if they tripped over it! To suggest that such people acted "in a moral way"! They do not know how!

On the other hand, the journalist comes close to the truth, when he refers to the "movement" as a "democratic awakening", which is "difficult to distill to a few demands". In fact, all Revolutions are characterized by the fact that common people get into motion, not aware of that which they are doing. For that reason, their demands were "difficult to distill".

The fact of the matter is that the Occupy Movement was absolutely Revolutionary! Countless people, those who were "formerly apathetic", become "politically active". Or as those who took part in the Occupy Movement phrased it, they "woke up".

This is characteristic of all Revolutions. Lenin went into this, in detail, in his excellent article, Left Wing Communism, An Infantile Disorder. That too, is required reading for all Revolutionaries.

To proceed with our analysis of the second paragraph. The reference to the slogan, "We are the 99%", is a reference to the fact that the "lower classes" were *beginning* to become *class conscious!* This calls for a little explanation.

It is a fundamental tenet of Marxism, that the working class is not aware of itself *as a class!* The conditions of life, of the working class, do not lead to that awareness! That awareness, that class consciousness, must be brought to the working class, from an outside source. That outside source 's middle class intellectuals, Scientific Socialists, which is to , Marx and Lenin.

Marx lived and worked in the mid to late nineteenth century, while capitalism was still in its pre monopoly stage, referred to as competitive capitalism. Through his scientific analysis of capitalism, he proved that it inevitably gave rise to Socialism. This is referred to as Scientific Socialism, which includes the Dictatorship of the Proletariat.

By contrast, there are a great many well meaning people who think that socialism is a good idea, even if it is "not likely". They are referred to as "utopian Socialists". They are about to receive a "rude awakening"!

At the "turn of the century", which is to say the end of the nineteenth century, and the beginning of the twentieth century, capitalism reached the stage of monopoly. Monopoly capitalism is technically referred to as "imperialism". Naturally, the monopoly capitalists are referred to as "imperialists". That merely stands to reason.

Lenin conducted a thorough examination of capitalism, in its monopoly stage, that of imperialism. He found that imperialism has characteristics which are different from capitalism in its early, competitive stage. He documented this in one of his greatest works, titled Imperialism, the Highest Stage of Capitalism.

In contrast to competitive capitalism, monopoly capitalism, imperialism, has *absolutely no progressive characteristics!* As Lenin phrased it, it is *"reaction, right down the line!"* That is another book that I consider to be essential, in the development of a proper Scientific Socialist, a true Communist.

To return to Russia, in early 1917, immediately after the Czar had been overthrown. The capitalists immediately established a democratic republic, under their rule, of course. This is referred to as the dictatorship of the bourgeoisie. A fool, by the name of Kerensky, was the "figure head" they placed in charge. This gave birth to the short lived Kerensky Regime.

For the common people of Russia, the workers and peasants, not a great deal changed. The great slaughter of working people, referred to as the First World War, continued. They remained cold and hungry, used as "cannon fodder" by the military commanders. The land which was promised to the peasants, remained in the hands of the landlords. The Constituent Assembly was another promise that was never kept.

Under the Kerensky Regime, the Russian people were no longer being crushed and exploited by the Czar and the capitalists. They were "merely" being crushed and exploited by the capitalists! Not a vast improvement!

That situation is similar to the one we are living in now. Whereas in Russia, the working people were veterans of the Revolution of Oh Five, here in America, the working people are veterans of the Occupy Movement.

One important difference is that, in Russia at that time, there was a Communist Party, led by Lenin. The members of the Communist Party were able to explain, to the common people, the fact that the capitalists have to be overthrown. Further, the state apparatus, which has been set up by the capitalists, with the sole purpose of crushing the working people, must be smashed. It must be then replaced with another state apparatus, with the sole purpose of crushing the capitalists. This state apparatus is known as the Dictatorship of the Proletariat.

Incidentally, the Dictatorship of the Proletariat is a basic tenet of Marxism. In fact, it is the "touchstone" of a true Marxist. Only those who embrace the Dictatorship of the Proletariat are Marxists.

Yet the fact that we do not have a proper Communist Party, is no reason for despair. We have a cultured working class, and the Internet. Most working people have computers and know how to use them, or can find someone to help them. (I rely heavily on my grandchildren)

Revolutionary literature can now be downloaded from the Internet. Also, Revolutionary books are readily available, ordered from outlets on the Internet. Now it is a simple matter of reading those Revolutionary works, by Marx and Lenin. In that way, working people can become true Revolutionaries. There is no other way!

It is clear that the Revolutionary motion is once again sweeping the world. The press reports confirm this. Here is a sample, of headlines taken within the last few days, starting with the country of China:

"There are protests and defiance across China, against zero covid policy. There is a heavy police presence. Thousands risk safety protesting over covid lockdown. There is widespread fury and frustration. Shanghai is traumatized. All of China is fed up. There are protests in at least ten cities. Hong Kong is protesting. Chinese police are checking cell phones, in a bid to crush mass protests. Protesters in Guangzhou clash with riot police. The largest cell phone factory in the world is now shut down. The largest chip manufacturing company is now shut down. The riot police are seen across the country. A fire in Xinjiang killed ten people, in part because of covid restrictions. The unrest is the worst in thirty years."

It is perhaps not too surprising that the American press is quite concerned with the "unrest" in China. After all, the American capitalists have invested a great deal of capital in that country. Even though the press documents the squalid conditions of life within those factories, the journalists are more worried about a possible shortage of cell phones!

The United Nations is also making headlines:

"The United Nations says the cost of living crisis is the worst the world has experienced so far in the twenty first century. An estimated seventy one million more people are now living in poverty. There is no clear solution. There is civil unrest around the world."

The United Nations is correct when they say that the "cost of living is the worst the world has experienced in the twenty first century". They are also correct when they refer to "civil unrest around the world". They are careful to not mention the dreaded "R word", that of Revolution!

On the other hand, they are absolutely mistaken when they state that "There is no clear solution". There is a "clear solution". That clear solution is Scientific Socialism! That is only possible through Revolution, the overthrow of the capitalists, and the Dictatorship of the Proletariat! But then, they are also careful to not mention the word "capitalism"!

Then there are the headlines which refer to the strike movement:

"Strikes are becoming ever more common, from truck drivers in Chile and South Korea, to rail workers and nurses in the United Kingdom. Industrial unrest is spreading across large areas of the world. A global cost of living crisis is pushing workers to go on strike. The unions in South Korea are excessively strong, so the government is determined to break the truckers strike. The striking truckers in Chile are holding their ground. The truckers in Chile walked out of talks."

Please note that here too, the term "industrial unrest" is used, instead of Revolution! The bourgeois journalists have so many creative ways of avoiding the word Revolution!

"The rising cost of living is leading to global unrest. Economies barely recovering from the pandemic are now facing more hardship. The war in Ukraine, climate crisis, cost of fuel, food and fertilizer, have pushed several countries beyond their ability to cope. Farmers and truck drivers are feeling the impact. Around the world, workers are demanding better pay and working conditions."

Now we can add the term "global unrest" to our list of expressions the bourgeois journalists use, instead of Revolution!

"In London, the scale of unrest is mounting. No one has seen anything like it. Teachers, postal workers, and others are going on strike. A winter of discontent is predicted. They are no closer to a solution."

This writer "hit the nail right on the head"! It is true when he says, they are "no closer to a solution". Because there is no solution! Not under capitalism! Socialism is required, but then that requires a Revolution! Followed by the Dictatorship of the Proletariat!

It seems clear that the Revolutionary Movement is now raging around the world. Just as the Occupy Movement quickly spread around the world, in a matter of *days*, so too this current Revolution is spreading, almost as quickly. It has very likely already "touched down on the shores" of America. The Truckers Protest of several months ago, may well be regarded as the beginning of the American Socialist Revolution.

That is a mere selection of the topics that are being reported, mainly on foreign news outlets. There are numerous others, all concerning Revolutionary motion, in various countries. The American press tends to ignore such topics.

It is very likely that this will end up being a World Socialist Revolution. The Revolution is raging in so many highly industrialized countries! As well as a number of countries which are not so highly industrialized!

It is not by chance that the press is reporting so many strikes by truckers and railroads. Most Revolutions start in the transportation industry!

Now on the "home front", a possible railroad strike could happen very soon. In response, President Biden, a self declared "friend of the Unions", has just declared an "imposed labour agreement". He proposed a law, passed by both Houses of Congress, which forces the Railroad Unions to accept the contract, which they voted down! Some friend of the Unions!

It remains to be seen if the railroad workers will stay on the job, or defy the government order to keep working.

The Revolutionary motion is becoming ever stronger, in ever more countries of the world, on a daily basis. Yet the American journalists remain quite complacent. Perhaps that is a reflection of the attitude of the politicians. It is entirely possible that they are oblivious to the Revolutionary storm that is about to wash over the country.

There is an expression to the effect that "Nero fiddled while Rome burned". If there was ever an occasion when that was applicable, it is now. It is quite possible that the trains will soon quit moving. If that happens, it is very likely that the truckers will join them. Also the airline workers. For a start. Revolution!

So what are the politicians concerned with? The next Speaker of the House! The 2024 presidential election, still two years away! Volcano in Hawaii! Madness!

Yet this is perhaps typical. Immediately before the common people of France broke down the walls of the castles of the Nobility, the nobles were squabbling among themselves, gossiping and planning their next balls. The Revolution caught them completely unaware! Even though it had been building up for many years!

Perhaps the American billionaires are similar to the French nobility. They may be unable to even imagine a world in which they are not the rulers! It is entirely possible, that they cannot imagine the idea of losing their wealth and power! The idea of a Socialist American Revolution, of being crushed under the Dictatorship of the Proletariat, may never have crossed their minds!

A more recent Revolution, one that is more pertinent, was the third Russian Revolution of the twentieth century, on October 25, OSC, or November 7, NSC. It was led by Lenin and the Bolsheviks, as that was the name by which they referred to themselves. It was well organized and almost bloodless. The Kerensky Regime was overthrown. The state apparatus was smashed. It was replaced by the Dictatorship of the Proletariat. The first Soviet Socialist Republic was born.

The next American Socialist Revolution should follow the example of that October Revolution. But then that is true for most of the highly industrialized countries of the world. Yet each country is different, so that the Revolutionary leaders of each country will have to devise an appropriate course of action.

The next few weeks should prove to be critical for the World Socialist Revolution. Events are happening at breakneck speed. Revolution could take place in any number of countries, giving rise to Socialist Republics.

I can once again stress the importance of becoming familiar with Revolutionary literature. If nothing else, by all means study State and Revolution. Imperialism, the Highest Stage of Capitalism. What Is To Be Done? and Left Wing Communism, An Infantile Disorder. All written by Lenin. All supremely relevant. I can think of no better way to prepare for the Revolution.

It is entirely possible that we may soon be facing that which Lenin foresaw:

World Socialist Republic

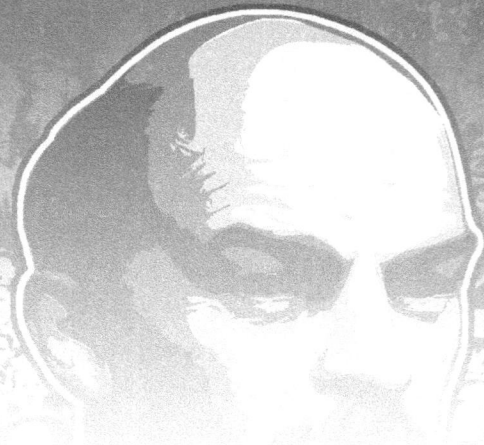

# CHAPTER 10

## World Socialist Republic

On September 16, 2022, Mahsa Amini, a twenty two year old Iranian woman, died while in the hospital, as a result of head injuries. This young lady was first arrested, by the "morality police", for the terrible "crime" of not wearing her head scarf (hajib) properly. Part of her hair was still visible! She was then taken to jail, beaten and died of her wounds.

It is entirely possible that this day will go down in history, as the beginning of the World Socialist Revolution.

Almost immediately, protests erupted and quickly spread all across Iran. Women of all ages began to burn their head scarfs and cut their hair. As well, marches and demonstrations have taken place, across the country. The police have tried very hard to quell the protests, with a great many protesters being arrested, while others have been killed, but to no avail. Instead, these protests have spread around the world. Even the journalists are now referring to this as a full scale Revolution.

Comparisons with the first Russian Revolution of 1917, referred to as the February Revolution, come to mind. The similarities are striking. For one thing, Iran is a big country, and while it is nowhere near the size of Russia, it is still about three times the size of France. As well, the current government of Iran states that "Irans Republican and Islamic foundations are inextricably linked together Constitutionally".

The implication is that there are two sets of laws, which are "inextricably linked together". On the one hand, there are the laws of the Republic of Iran, the "laws of man", and on the other hand, there are the Islamic Foundation laws, the "Laws of God"! In other words, the "laws of man" are "inextricable linked together" with the "laws of God"! Those two laws were never meant to be "linked together"!

Under a democratic republic, no monarch is recognized, and citizens have certain democratic rights. One of those democratic rights is that of worshiping the God of our understanding, as we see fit. No one, and certainly no government, has any right to impose their beliefs on any citizen! Yet by "linking together" the laws of the Republic with the Islamic Foundation laws, that is precisely what is happening!

The people of Iran are going to have to separate the two! No doubt the Revolutionary uprising is determined to separate the laws of the Islamic Foundation, from the laws of the Republic of Iran.

By comparison with Russia in early 1917, the common people of Russia were being crushed by the nobility and the capitalists. By the "common people" I am referring to the workers and the peasants. The power of the Czar was almost absolute, while the conditions of life for the working class people was deplorable. The peasants in turn were also exploited by the landlords. All were cold, hungry and being used as "cannon fodder" in the war with Germany and the Central Powers. They wanted nothing so much as bread, peace and land. The Czar and the capitalists had no intention of giving them any of that. I should add that by "capitalists", I am referring to the monopoly capitalists, at that time referred to as millionaires, not those who own a small business.

Yet as is well known, the Revolution became so strong that in February of 1917, Czar Nicholas was overthrown. The three hundred year long reign of the Romanovs was finished! The common people of Russia had accomplished the impossible! No one thought this was possible! The power of Revolution!

Now it is up to the common people of Iran, the workers and peasants, to also overturn the laws of the Islamic Foundation. By that, I mean to get the clergy out of the business of governing! Religion has no place in politics! The Iranian Republic must separate from the Islamic Foundation!

Assuming that takes place, then the situation will be similar to that which existed in Russia, after the Czar was overthrown. A Russian democratic republic was established, with the class of capitalists in power. At that time, the capitalists placed a self proclaimed socialist, a fool by the name of Kerensky, as the figure head leader, a mere puppet of the capitalists. The land remained in the hands of the landlords, the war continued, the promised Constituent Assembly was delayed, and all the common people, both workers and peasants, remained as cold and hungry as eve still used as cannon fodder, all truly desperate.

Yet the Czar was no longer in power, and that was a s in the right direction. The next step, that of overthrow the capitalists, required the direction of Scientific Sociali

The common people had gone as far as they could. The hated Czar was overthrown. By themselves, they could do no more. They needed a leader.

In April of that year, their leader returned from exile. His name was Vladimir Ilyich Ulyanov, commonly known as Lenin.

It was Lenin who explained to the common people the necessity of Revolution. He pointed out that the class of people who were running the country, the capitalists, technically known as the bourgeoisie, had to be overthrown. They are concerned only with their profit. Just as a Revolution was required, to overthrow the Czar, so too another Revolution was required, to overthrow the capitalists.

The Russian working class was not aware of this, for good reason. The working class, the proletariat, is not aware of itself, as a class. The conditions of life, of the proletariat, do not lead to this awareness. That awareness must be brought to the working class, from an outside source. That outside source is middle class intellectuals. Make no mistake, Marx and Lenin were middle class intellectuals.

Lenin worked all his life to raise the level of awareness of the working class, to make them "class conscious". There is a reason for this. It is the working class, the proletariat, that is a truly Revolutionary class. Even though in Russia, at that time, they were in a minority, it was up to them to *lead* the Revolution, against the capitalists, to victory. This they accomplished, in magnificent style, in October of 1917.

Now a similar situation exists, and not just in Iran, but around the world. Just as the working class of Russia was not aware of itself as a class, with its own class interests, so too the working class, the proletariat, of other countries of today, are not class conscious.

In Russia, in 1917, Lenin and other Communists, provided the working people of Russia with the class consciousness they so desperately needed. Now it is up to middle class intellectuals of today, to provide the working class Revolutionaries, of all countries of the world, with that class consciousness.

There are a few important differences between Russia of 1917, and the present. Not the least of which is the fact that currently, we have no true Communist Party. Or at least, none of which I am aware. Certainly there is no Communist Party in any highly industrialized country of the world. Bear in mind that a true Communist Party embraces the Dictatorship of the Proletariat, the "touchstone" of a true Marxist, according to Lenin.

Mind you, there is no shortage of Parties which claim to be Marxist. Social chauvinists, one and all, those who are Socialists in words, chauvinists in deeds. They are all "revisionists", those who try to "revise" the Revolutionary theories of Marx and Lenin. They are among the most dedicated, devoted servants of the billionaires, the capitalists. Belly crawling boot lickers, one and all.

Then too, we have the self described Democratic Socialists, those who are fighting for democracy and Socialism. We have no quarrel with these people, as they make no claim to be Marxists. These are our friends and allies.

The point being that it is now up to people who are aware of the Revolutionary theories of Marx and Lenin, to raise the level of awareness of the common people. Further, not just in America, but around the world. As the fires of Revolution are raging, in perhaps all of the industrialized countries of the world, the need is immediate and urgent.

All working people, and especially the proletariat, must be made aware of themselves as a class, with their own class interests. The class of people in charge, the capitalists, the billionaires, the bourgeoisie, must be overthrown. This can only happen through Revolution. Further, the state apparatus, which has been set up to crush the working people, must be smashed. It must then be replaced with a different state apparatus, one which is designed to crush the capitalists, as they try desperately to restore their "paradise lost". This working class state apparatus is known as the Dictatorship of the Proletariat.

Lenin explained this supremely well in his excellent article, State and Revolution. That is required reading for all Revolutionaries.

With respect to the current Revolution taking place in Iran, as well as in other countries of the world, may I suggest that we learn from the experience of previous Revolutions. In particular, the Russian Revolutions, as they so closely resemble our own. We can learn from their successes, as well as their mistakes.

At the time of the Russian Revolution, about three quarters of the people were peasants. The conditions of life, of the peasants, do not lead to the awareness of the necessity of Revolution. It is also very likely that few of them could read. Yet the situation was desperate, and under the leadership of the working class, the proletariat, a great many peasants became Revolutionary. That is especially true of the poor peasants.

As previously mentioned, at that time, Russia was blessed with a true Communist Party. The members of this Party were most valuable in raising the level of awareness of the common people, both workers and peasants.

Another important difference of today, which can work in our favour, is the fact that the working people of Iran are now quite "cultured". According to the Internet, in this country of possibly 85 million people, around 80 percent of the men, and 65 percent of the women, are literate. Excellent! No doubt many of those people have digital devices of some sort, generally referred to as computers. These can be used to download Revolutionary literature from the Internet.

That is also very likely the case in various other countries of the world, where Revolution is raging, especially in the most highly industrialized countries.

There is currently wide spread support, in various countries of the world, especially concerning the Revolution in Iran. No doubt the people of Iran speak various languages, although Farsi is predominant. So I suggest that people in other countries support these Revolutionaries, by sending Revolutionary literature in their own language. State and Revolution is absolutely critical. Other important works of Lenin include What Is To Be Done?, Imperialism, the Highest Stage of Capitalism, and Left Wing Communism, An Infantile Disorder.

It is significant that the Iranian Revolution is being led by women and students. In North America, the women and students are also playing a key role. No doubt many women, and almost all students, are familiar with the Revolutionary theories of Marx and Lenin. Equally without doubt, all are determined to "make a difference". Now is your chance! Get together with people from Iran, or of Iranian descent, and make contact with the Revolutionaries in Iran, through the Internet, of course. Support them in any way possible, especially with Revolutionary literature, in a language they understand.

WORLD SOCIALIST REVOLUTION

The Revolutionaries of Iran are in the forefront of the Revolutionary Movement, soon to become part of a World Socialist Revolution. They are not the only ones! China is also in "turmoil", to use the expression of the bourgeois. The Chinese censors are doing their best to keep all reports on the protests, secret from the world, but the occasional email does get through. There are also wide spread protests in Russia. As I write this, Peru is "in the news". Apparently the whole country is in a "state of anarchy".

Clearly, the Revolution is spreading around the world. The Revolutionaries of all those countries need our help, and not just those in Iran. Very soon the Revolution will touch down on the shores of North America. It is about to become part of a World Socialist Revolution!

The fact of the matter is that the monopoly capitalists, the billionaires, the bourgeoisie, are supremely well aware of this. They are an exceptionally class conscious group of people! They recognize this Revolutionary Movement, while carefully avoiding the word Revolution. At the same time, they go to great lengths, resort to verbal gymnastics, in an effort to avoid the use of the word "Revolution", as well as the word "capitalism"!

We are currently experiencing a "crisis in capitalism", and the capitalists admit that they "have no solutions". Yet the Obama duo have recently set up the "Obama Foundation", with the goal of "finding a cure". We can only marvel at such starry eyed optimism! They honestly think that they can "fix" capitalism!

Having said that, allow me to add that I believe in "giving credit where credit is due". I have to say that the Obama Foundation certainly has a done a fine job of pointing out the problem, as well as the solution! At the same time, they were careful to make *no mention of Revolution!* For that matter, they made *no mention of classes!*

In fact, they "hit the nail on the head", with this statement: "ordinary people working together can change history"! True! In fact, it is a fundamental tenet of Marxism that "the masses are the makers of history"!

It gets even better when they go on to say: "Our mission is to inspire those people to take action, empower them to change their world for the better, and connect them so they can achieve more together than they can alone"!

Outstanding! To think that the Obama Foundation is encouraging people to do precisely the same thing that I am recommending! By all means, get together and change the world! Take action! Unite with Revolutionaries in other parts of the world! The one and only way the world can be changed for the better, is by overthrowing international capital! Take to heart the immortal words of Marx, and *Unite With the Workers of the World!*

Here in North America, the capitalists are trying desperately to "hold it together". Inflation is out of control, gun violence is widespread, drug overdoses are common place, the number of homeless are increasing, the food banks are running out of food, the trains may quit running, and the country may soon shut down, possibly facing bankruptcy. So what is the response of the politicians in Washington? They are in gridlock, fighting among themselves! Rather than face the problems of today, they are focused on the federal election of two years hence!

For the benefit of those who are just now becoming politically active, may I point out that this is merely capitalism, in a state of crisis. The finest bourgeois economists admit that they cannot see any solution. But then they cannot imagine a world of socialism. Yet they are able to *describe it!*

In fact, one of the finest of the bourgeois economists, a man who was formerly the Chairman of the Council of Economic Advisors under President Obama, stated the problem quite clearly, while working for the Obama Foundation. His "solution", to the current crisis in capitalism, was to suggest "approaches and solutions that are responsive to citizens and create inclusive and equitable economic realities for everyone".

To think that one of the finest bourgeois economists suggested "inclusive and equitable economic realities for everyone"! To put this in simple terms, that is called *Socialism!* He just made the argument for Socialism, without realizing this! In fact, he refers to this as "inclusive capitalism"! Reality check, dear fellow! *Socialism* is just that! *Socialism!* Referring to this as "inclusive capitalism" does not change the fact that it is *Socialism!*

As strange as this may seem, it is quite common! In his article, Left Wing Communism, An Infantile Disorder, Lenin quoted a statement by the British Prime Minister, Lloyd George. That statement, by the Prime Minister, made absolutely no sense! As Lenin then stated, "this argument shows in particular how muddled even the most intelligent members of the bourgeoisie have become, and how they cannot help committing irreparable blunders. That, in fact, is what will bring about the downfall of the bourgeoisie."

That explains the "peculiar behaviour" of this highly respected bourgeois economist! Even though he is one of the "most intelligent" of the lot, he is truly "muddled".

Perhaps someone should explain to this simple soul, this top bourgeois economist, that he is misguided! The Fundamental Law of Capitalism -assuming such a law exists- is that *sentiment has no monetary value!* All billionaires are supremely well aware of this! All attempts to "tug on their heart strings" are futile, as they do not have any! Each and every one of them is a highly successful psycho path!

It is significant that another name for "inclusive capitalism" is "woke capitalism". Apparently the word "woke" is a reference to the idea that capitalists "have a conscience". *Nonsense!* Capitalists have about as much conscience as snakes have feathers!

It is significant that certain journalists, those who are the strongest supporters of capitalism, and in particular those of Fox News, ridicule the idea of "woke corporations" and "woke capitalism". Properly so! The sole purpose of capitalism is to make a profit! They refer to this as their "bottom line"! Conscience be damned! Whatever it takes to "make a buck"!

Yet even though capitalism has reached a state of crisis, around the world, the system will not collapse, under its own weight. It has to be smashed!

With that in mind, the fact is that Councils, otherwise known as Soviets, appear spontaneously, or "pop up", during a time of Revolution. By all means, become involved with those Councils. Take part in training people for the approaching Insurrection. Organize study groups with Marxist literature. Make such literature widely available. Use the Internet and social media to carry the message. In America, join the two mainstream political parties, Democrat and Republican, as card carrying members. Coordinate Revolutionary actions with other Councils, and with Revolutionaries of other countries. Those who are familiar with the Revolutionary theories of Marx and Lenin can work towards forming a Communist Party, one which calls for the Dictatorship of the Proletariat. We can expect the most advanced workers to also take part in creating a true Communist Party, in various countries of the world, as they become aware of those Revolutionary theories.

The fact of the matter is that most of the people who are leading this World Socialist Revolution, at least in Iran and in America, are women and students. That is very likely also the case in other countries of the world. That places a huge burden on their shoulders. That is not the way it should be. The men should be leading the Revolution. No doubt as the Revolution grows in strength, countless men will become active. Until then, it is up to women and students to "blaze the trail". I deeply regret that. Yet there is *no other way!* But then, quite recently, it was women and students who proved to be excellent organizers. For that reason, I have complete confidence in them.

As for those who think that perhaps I am overstating the case, bear in mind that Revolutions tend to spread, and rapidly. That which the press is referring to as "social upheaval" is Revolution, happening now, in various parts of the world. I consider this to be the beginning of a full scale World Socialist Revolution. I fully expect it to spread across the world. A World Socialist Revolution, which will in turn give rise to a World Socialist Republic.

No doubt, some may argue that the Revolution may not be Socialist. To such people, I can only respond that we live in a class society. We live under the rule of the capitalists. The capitalists are in charge. This is referred to as the dictatorship of the bourgeoisie. The one and only alternative is Socialism, the Dictatorship of the Proletariat. There is no middle course. No one in his right mind wants to continue to live under capitalism. Aside from the billionaires, of course. And they are not about to take part in any Revolution!

We will know that we are successful, when the term Dictatorship of the Proletariat is common place, when common people are openly calling for a Communist Party, for Socialism, and an end to capitalism.

May I suggest to the people who are now protesting, that they become more creative. Feel free to harass the capitalists, and their political servants, in various ways. Make their lives as miserable as possible. Create disturbances at their homes and businesses. Go to their restaurants and disrupt their fancy meals. Hound them at their vacation resorts. Sing to them the Internationale! Give them no peace! Protesters who have experience in entertainment, can no doubt devise methods of protest which are not only annoying, but also entertaining. Such events tend to make the evening news! Perhaps even the late night entertainment shows! In this way, the bourgeois journalists will assist us in spreading the message. Ever more working people will become politically aware. Bear in mind, that the best way to educate, is by entertaining, at the same time!

Make sure that banners and signs are placed in public locations, for all to see. These may read:

Workers of the World, Unite!

Dictatorship of the Proletariat!

Soviet Power!

Scientific Socialism!

World Socialist Republic!

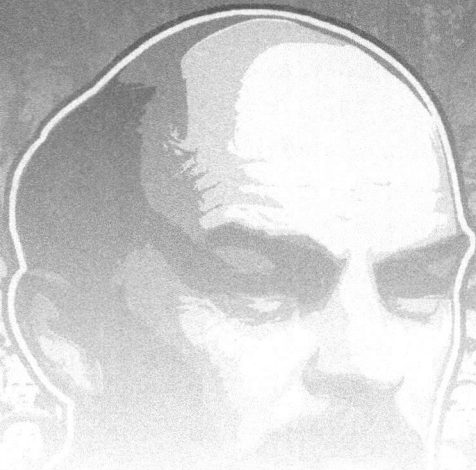

# CHAPTER 11

## Freedom Convoy 2023

A spokesman, for an organization known as Canada Unity, has just announced plans for a "Freedom Convoy 2.0. This is also being referred to as a "World Unity Convoy". The plan is to gather in Winnipeg, Manitoba, from February 17-20, 2023. This "reunion" is to start on the anniversary of the last day that the truckers occupied Ottawa, on February 17, 2022.

The original "Freedom Convoy", of 2022, was billed as a "protest against the Covid 19 vaccine mandates, public health protections, and the Liberal Government generally". The organizers even came up with a "Memorandum of Understanding", MOU, that "called on the Governor General and the Senate to form a committee with Convoy protesters to end all Covid 19 health protections nation wide." This MOU was later withdrawn, if for no other reason than the fact that carrying out that demand, is simply not possible! The Governor General and the Senate do not have that authority! Such is only possible through the House of Commons!

The leaders of Canada Unity say that the Freedom Convoy to Winnipeg would focus on "solutions for a better world for all Canadians". He claims that the city of Ottawa was "hostile to them". Imagine that! He wants their "voices to be loud but safe". The proposed plan is for a three day gathering, to include a "peaceful, multi day assembly, featuring speeches, ceremonies, events and guest speakers." That sounds very similar to a religious gathering! Yet the working people need Revolution, not religion!

A lady, who posted a separate video on the Canada Unity page, said "The goal is to facilitate a grass roots movement of citizens world wide". Another possible leader of Canada Unity had more to add: "The simple fact is that we can't have Unity without Reconciliation which has to come from 'We the People', and not from our Government. Let's be grown up and start addressing the root of division, discrimination and segregation in Canada by changing our focus away from division to that of one word, 'Unity'".

All of the aforementioned is consistent with their "Vision and Mission" statement, posted on July 17, 2022:

"Who We Are:

"Our Vision is to advocate, educate and participate in awareness campaigns, to restore and preserve Canadians Constitutional right to be free from government overreach.

"Our Mission is to successfully hold the Government accountable for the rule of law and end all mandates. We stand together with our countrymen impacted by these illegal policies and fight for justice, reckoning and restitution."

First, allow me to make it clear that the leaders of Canada Unity are technically referred to as "bourgeois democrats". They are focused on "patching up the system", and in particular, in defending our democratic rights. Nothing wrong with that! They are determined to unite people. They are careful to make no mention of classes. As "our countrymen" include capitalists, then their idea is to "unite" with the capitalists!

These Unity Canada leaders, as bourgeois democrats, are the "natural and desirable allies" of the working class, according to Lenin. Those of us who are Marxists, currently referred to as Communists, have no problem with bourgeois democrats! We would like nothing so much as to work *with* them!

Having said that, an essential condition for such an alliance must be complete liberty for us, the Marxists, the Communists, to reveal to the working class that its interests are diametrically opposed to the interests of the monopoly capitalists, the billionaires, those who are technically referred to as the bourgeoisie. There can be no question of "Unity" with the capitalists!

For the purpose of this article, I simply refer to the billionaires as capitalists. They are not to be confused with the small business owners, technically referred to as the petty bourgeois. They too are the natural allies of the working class, the Proletariat.

Now to the heart of the matter, the Truckers Protest. The fact of the matter is that last year, these protests spread all across Canada, and to America, so that the movement is very broad and deep. Yet it is still largely spontaneous. The drivers are well aware that there is strength in numbers, and further, that there is a certain antagonism between workers and employers. Yet that is a far cry from being aware of themselves as members of a class, with their own class interests.

The truckers are not to be blamed for this! No worker is aware of this, as the conditions of life of the working class, do not lead to that awareness! That awareness can be brought to workers only from an outside source! That outside source is middle class intellectuals. In particular, Marx and Lenin!

Ideally, it is up to Members of a true Communist Party, to carry the message to the working people, including the truckers. Yet as we have no true Communist Party, at least not here in North America, it is up to the members of the working class, to educate themselves.

In years gone by, this was almost impossible. Not now! Now most working people can read. Further, a great many of them have computers, or digital devices of some sort. The younger workers especially, know how to use them! The capitalists have thoughtfully provided us with the Internet, with which we can down load various Revolutionary works of literature, as well as order Marxist books. As most workers also have credit cards, that is not difficult.

As mentioned in previous articles, the most important Revolutionary book now, is State and Revolution, by Lenin. Then too, there is Imperialism, the Highest Stage of Capitalism, What Is To Be Done?, and Left Wing Communism, An Infantile Disorder, all written by Lenin. As well, the Communist Manifesto, by Marx and Engels, can easily be downloaded from the Internet. A careful reading of those Revolutionary works will provide workers with a fine grounding in Revolutionary Marxism, otherwise known as Communism.

I stress the importance of State and Revolution, as it is so relevant. Whether people know it or not, and most do not know it, we are leading up to a Revolution. It is just a matter of time before the Insurrection takes place. At that time, the working people will seize power. Right then and there, the state apparatus, which has been set up to crush the working class, must be *smashed!* Otherwise, the leaders of the Revolution will take over the state apparatus, and set themselves up *as the new rulers!* That is the last thing we need!

After the existing state apparatus is destroyed, a new state apparatus must be set up, in the form of the Dictatorship of the Proletariat. A Dictatorship is just that, a Dictatorship! The capitalists will have no rights! The "shoe will be on the other foot"! We will see how they like it! They will make every attempt to regain their wealth and power, to restore their "paradise lost"! And we, the working class, the Proletariat, will not allow that! The days of hiding behind high priced lawyers will soon be over!

It is very likely that the workers will then establish workers courts, possibly in the form of a team of three workers, to act as judges. These may be referred to as tribunals. The ruling of these tribunals will be final. There will be no court of appeal.

That which applies to the capitalists, also applies to the criminals. They will be crushed. Their days are numbered! The sex offenders and pedophiles will be held accountable! The dope dealers will have to answer for all the overdoses they have caused! The mobsters will learn the meaning of the word Dictatorship! The days of being mollycoddled in a "correctional institution" will soon be over! They are about to learn the restorative value of manual labour!

The bourgeois democrats call for "Unity". Of course, they have every right to do just that. Yet such a call ignores the fact that we live in a class society. There can be no question of "uniting" with the capitalists! We are class enemies!

In the work by Lenin, What Is To Be Done?, he stresses the fact that we live in a class society. Bourgeois and Proletarian! One or the other! There is no middle ground! Either bourgeois or Proletarian ideology! As we live in a society torn by class antagonisms, there can never be a "non class" or "above class" ideology. The point is that "to belittle socialist ideology *in any way,* to *deviate from it in the slightest degree,* means strengthening bourgeois ideology.... the *spontaneous* development of the labour movement leads to its becoming subordinated to bourgeois ideology...pure and simple trade unionism... and trade unionism means the ideological enslavement of the workers to the bourgeoisie". (italics by Lenin)

It is clear that as long as working people have the ideology of the capitalists, the bourgeois, then they will continue to fight for better wages, working conditions, and even democratic rights. Nothing more! This is referred to as "trade unionism". This is fine, as far as it goes! It does not go far enough! We do not need paltry reforms! We need Revolution! The working people must be made aware of this!

It is very likely that the truckers will be in motion in early February. This is not to say that the truckers should go to Winnipeg for three days of "speeches, ceremonies and guest speakers", seeking "solutions for a better world for all Canadians". There is no need to "seek these solutions"! We already know the solution! Socialism! Through Revolution! The Dictatorship of the Proletariat!

It is very likely that Councils were active during the Truckers Protest in Ottawa. I say this because Revolution gives rise to Councils, otherwise known as Soviets. Plus the fact that the occupation of downtown Ottawa was supremely well organized. That is only possible through Councils! Now is the time for those Councils to become ever more active.

As mentioned in a previous article, it is very likely that the Canadian capitalists will agree to a "buy out". That is far preferable to a violent Revolution. According to Lenin, the four conditions, which are necessary for a non violent Revolution, exist in Canada. These are a cultured Proletariat, a Proletariat in the majority, strong unions, and a ruling class which is accustomed to rule through a process of compromise. Faced with the proper motivation, it is very likely that the Canadian capitalists will soon become "sweetly reasonable".

That proper motivation may well come from the truckers, as well as those who support them. Perhaps the most important support, of the Truckers Protest, can come from the railroad workers. Assuming the trucks and the trains go on strike, then the country will soon, almost immediately, come to a stand still! That is sure to get the immediate, undivided attention of the capitalists!

It is no secret that the railroad workers are not at all happy! With good reason, I might add! Their working conditions are deplorable, and the government just forced a contract "down their throats"! A contract the workers voted down, I might add! Legislated back to work!

Now is the time for the Councils, which have taken shape around the Truckers, to get together with the Councils which have taken shape around the railroad workers. An Insurrection is critical, but timing is all important! The Insurrection can be successful, *only* if the vast majority of working people support a Revolution! In fact, get together with as many Councils as possible! The level of discontent of the common people must be accurately gauged! Not just in Canada, but also in America.

The bourgeois press is reporting that a great many common people, those who previously supported Trump and his followers, are now "moving to the Left", without stating it in those precise words. Yet it is very likely correct, as the journalists get paid to give an accurate report of such events.

Assuming the level of discontent is deep and wide spread, then it is time for the Insurrection. At such a time, it is necessary to act decisively! As Marx stated, "the defensive is the death of every Insurrection!" The capital must be occupied, as well as all major cities. The trains must be shut down, the major bridges and tunnels blocked. Who better to blockade than the trucks? The airports must be closed, as well as the sea ports. All government officials must be arrested, on a federal and provincial level. All communications networks must be secured.

It would be far better if an Insurrection, here in Canada, was coordinated with an Insurrection in America. The only difference is that there can be no talk of the American capitalists agreeing to a "buy out". That is not about to happen. By contrast, it is very likely that the Canadian capitalists will "resign themselves to their fate".

If the Insurrection is swift and well organized, as was the case in Russia, in 1917, then the bloodshed will be minimal.

It is to be hoped that the bourgeois democrats have learned a thing or two, since the Truckers Protest of last year. Since then, a mere few months ago, there has been considerable change. Inflation has sky rocketed! Far more people are now hungry! Many others are forced to choose between eating and having a roof over their heads! More food banks are now empty! More people are homeless! Drug overdoses are commonplace! Gun violence is routine! Now people are openly requesting assisted suicide! The suffering of the common people has now reached horrendous proportions!

The lesson to be learned, my bourgeois democratic friends, is that *half measures get us nowhere!* That includes demanding paltry reforms, such as the recognition of our democratic rights.

The point is that workers must be made aware of the Revolutionary theories of Marx and Lenin. They must become aware of themselves as the members of a class, that of Proletarians. They must be made aware of the fact that the capitalists are responsible for the current state of affairs, this "crisis in capitalism". The only solution is through Revolution, the smashing of the existing state apparatus, and establishing the Dictatorship of the Proletariat. There is *no other way!*

On the website of Canada Unity, the slogan "Hold the Line" was suggested, as well as "Freedom". Indeed, those slogans were repeated in the Truckers Protest, and not just in Ottawa. Yet neither slogan contains any class content! May I suggest a several different slogans, which contain class content:

Revolution!

Scientific Socialism!

Workers of the World, Unite!

Dictatorship of the Proletariat!

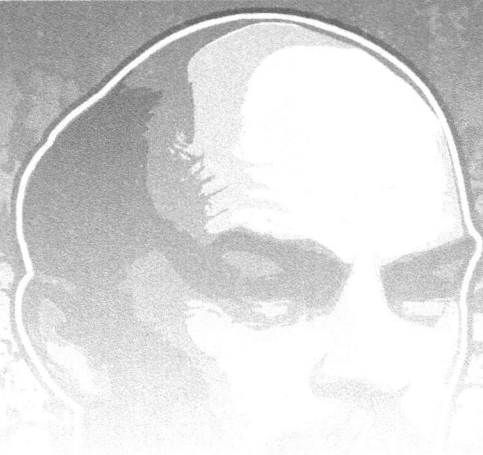

# CHAPTER 12

## Trump Facing Possible Criminal Charges

December 19, 2022. On that day, the Congressional January 6 Committee finally held their last "public meeting". After eighteen months of questioning witnesses, concerning the "January 6 Insurrection", of 2020, they have finally come to the conclusion that Trump very likely broke the law! Imagine that! They went to all that time and trouble to figure out that which everyone else already knows!

Now they are "recommending" to the Department of Justice that Trump, as well as his "associates", face "criminal prosecution".

In particular, they recommend that Trump be charged with four crimes:

1) Obstruction of an Official Proceeding of Congress
2) Assisting or Aiding An Insurrection

3) Conspiracy to Defraud the United States
4) Conspiracy to Make a False Statement

Citizens may well wonder the reason that a Congressional Committee would spend all that time and money, conduct a most thorough investigation, interview hundreds of people, gather mountains of documents, when there is nothing they can do with this! They do not have the authority to charge anyone! The best they can do is pass it off to a government agency, in this case the DOJ, whose job it is to investigate and prosecute possible crimes! Why bother? Why not just let the DOJ do the job they get paid to do?

The answer is contained in that most excellent article by Lenin, State and Revolution. As he points out, "the actual work of the 'state' is done behind the scenes and is carried on by the departments, the government offices and the General Staffs. Parliament itself is given up to talk for the purpose of fooling the 'common people'". (May I suggest that my American Comrades substitute the word Congress for Parliament)

All of that "talk", concerning the actions of a former president, was merely for the purpose of "fooling the common people". In terms of entertainment, it was quite a bore, along the lines of a second rate "soap opera". Yet the press was focused on this, and that served to distract people from the true "work of state", which was being done "behind the scenes".

In particular, the massive Omnibus Bill, which contains no less than 4,155 pages, was being prepared. This document, which involves funding the government for a year, at the expense of 1.7 *Trillion,* is several times bigger than the bible, and "was a result of haggling among *three lawmakers* who oversee Congressional appropriations", according to a journalist.

It is significant that almost *half* of the money goes towards the military. Even though countless people are going hungry, with the food banks running out of food, ever increasing numbers of people becoming homeless, those who have homes cannot afford to heat them, the medical system is on the verge of collapse, and the roads and bridges, the infrastructure of the country, are in the process of collapse! Yet the government can afford to spend *hundreds of billions on the military!*

The journalists are reporting that the Omnibus Bill is really composed of *twelve* spending bills! The "Party Bosses", those who work "behind the scenes", have thoughtfully relieved the politicians of the burden of voting on those separate bills. After all, they could even "get it wrong" and "vote the wrong way"! Perish forbid! This way, by combining all the Bills, they are "covering all the bases".

Now the Members of Congress, both in the House and in the Senate, are being pressured to pass this Omnibus Bill within three days! At that time, on December 23, the government will "hit the debt ceiling", or "run out of money", to put it in simple terms. Unless the Congress "raises the debt ceiling", so that they can borrow more money, the country will shut down. The politicians are determined to drive the country ever deeper into debt!

Also on that day, the Congress is scheduled to shut down, for the Christmas break. Now the lawmakers are faced with the choice of passing this Omnibus Bill, *of which they know nothing*, into law, or of voting against it, which would result in a government shut down.

Incidentally, an Omnibus Bill is a reference to the government spending for the next year. On the other hand,

WORLD SOCIALIST REVOLUTION

a Continuing Resolution, or CR, is a reference to the approval of spending for a rather short time, usually several weeks. This is commonly referred to as "kicking the can down the road".

It is doubtful that any Member of Congress will have a chance to read even a small part of that Bill. For that matter, it is even more doubtful that any Member of Congress will make any attempt to read that Bill! All of them understand that it is their job to "entertain" the common people, to make the appropriate speeches, while allowing the affairs of state to be tended to "behind the scenes". They also understand that it is now their "job" to "rubber stamp" this Omnibus Bill.

The divisions within the Republican Party, or GOP, Grand Old Party, as they refer to themselves, are now in the open. The Republican Members of the House are accusing the Senate Republicans of betraying them! They are even stooping to the childish behaviour of "name calling"!

The House Republicans want a short term Continuing Resolution, in order to keep the government going, at least until January 3. At that date, a new Congress will be sworn in, and the Republicans will have a majority in the House. That will give the House Republicans far more power. They are only too anxious to use that power!

Yet the Omnibus Bill passed the Senate, as a number of Senate Republicans voted in favour! As the Democrats control the House, the Bill is almost certain to pass.

On January 3, the day a new Congress officially convenes, it is almost certain that Kevin McCarthy will be elected as the next Speaker of the House. The journalists are reporting that he previously warned the Senate Republicans that if they passed the Omnibus Bill, then any Bills from the Senate, after he becomes Speaker, will arrive in the House, "DOA, Dead On Arrival". To think that the leaders of the country would sink to such childish behaviour!

It was only rather recently that the GOP had a "Golden Rule", which they referred to as the "Eleventh Commandment": "Thou shall not criticize a fellow Republican". In fact, they took that "Commandment" quite seriously. Yet now that "Commandment" has gone the way of the dodo bird!

It is clear that the class of people who are running the country, the capitalists, the billionaires, the bourgeoisie, are having a difficult time "holding it together". Some of their devoted servants, within the confines of Washington, by whom I mean the elected officials, are showing signs of independence! The nerve of those people! Who do they think they are? Are they not aware that the Party Bosses arranged for their election?

It is also clear that the same class of billionaires has decided that Trump has to go. They have had enough of that boy! He was given the "hint" in the 2020 presidential election, which was carefully "fixed", but now he is determined to once again, occupy the Oval Office. Sterner measures are required!

Hence the reason for the charges that will -hopefully!- be levelled against the former president! Not that they are focused on sending that man to jail. They just want to secure a conviction, one which will ensure that he cannot run for any office. Especially not for president! They have in mind the Fourteenth Amendment to the Constitution.

No doubt the capitalists were trying to "kill two birds with one stone". On the one hand, to keep the common people occupied with the January 6 Investigation, so that they could prepare the Omnibus Bill, "behind the scenes". On the other hand, and at the same time, to discredit Trump, and even have him convicted of crimes, so that he can never again run for office. The Fourteenth Amendment to the Constitution provides for this. As it is so important, I have included the key section:

Section 3.

"No person shall be a Senator or Representative in Congress, or elector of President and Vice President, or hold any office, civil or military, under the United States, or under any state, who, having previously taken an oath, as a member of Congress, or as an officer of the United States, or as a member of any state legislature, or as an executive or judicial officer of any state, to support the Constitution of the United States, shall have engaged in insurrection or rebellion against the same, or given aid or comfort to the enemies thereof. But Congress may by a vote of two-thirds of each House, remove such disability."

The key part of this section is that which explicitly forbids anyone to "hold any office ...who has previously taken an oath...as an officer of the United States...to support the Constitution of the United States, shall have engaged in insurrection or rebellion against the same, or given aid or comfort to the enemies thereof".

Trump was formerly the President of the United States. As such, he took an oath to "preserve, protect and defend the Constitution of the United States". Now if he is convicted of any or all of the charges that are being recommended by the Congressional Committee, then he will not be allowed to run for president. For that matter, he will not be allowed to run for any office.

As for those who scoff at the idea of a man, such as Trump, a billionaire, going to jail, I can only respond that you are right. That is not about to happen. Yet that is not the reason for the "suggested" charges!

The class of capitalists who are running the country, technically referred to as the bourgeoisie, are determined to "bench" Trump! If he is convicted of even one of these crimes, then he cannot run for president! One more "loose cannon" secured!

No doubt, the lawyers who work for Trump, warned him of this. Those same lawyers are also well aware of the policy, of the law enforcement agencies, of not pressing any charges, against any candidate, who is running for the office of the presidency. Such a charge could "bias the voters", having an influence on the election. Imagine that!

Bear in mind that Trump is not entirely stupid. For that reason, immediately before the Congressional Committee released its "recommendations", that of charging Trump, he "threw his hat into the ring". Trump is once again running for President!

Bear in mind that there is a big difference between "policy" and "the law"! The "policy" of not charging any presidential candidates, is a far cry from the law! Trump can still be charged, even though he is now officially running for president! Yet the decision to charge him is considered to be a "hot potato"! Any Prosecutor who chooses to charge Trump is risking "career suicide"!

No one within the Justice Department is stupid enough to take such a gamble! In the interests of that which they refer to as "CYA", "Cover Your Ass", they have appointed a "Special Prosecutor". This is also referred to as "passing the buck"!

Now the decision, to charge Trump or not to charge Trump, "To be or not to be", is in the hands of a supremely brave man, one who has accepted this appointment. Mind you, some would add that he is also supremely stupid!

That is a matter of opinion. That which is not a matter of opinion, is the fact that the Revolution, or perhaps more accurately, the Revolutionary Motion, is growing ever stronger, around the world, and not just in America.

The results of the "midterm elections" are a clear indication of this. All of the "political pundits" were convinced that the Republicans would gain a huge majority in the House, as well as possibly a majority in the Senate. We now know that they managed to get a "razor thin" majority in the House. Nothing more. The Democrats still control the Senate.

In all fairness to those "political forecasters", they were not "reading tea leaves". The journalists especially, were spending a great deal of time talking to common people, the members of the public. To their surprise, they found that within a rather short period of time, the "mood" of those people has changed dramatically. In fact, those who were formerly rather strong supporters of Trump, as well as other "Right Wing" candidates for office, are now not so enthusiastic.

To put this in scientific terms, we can say that the "masses" -a term I hate!, as I prefer the expression "common people"-, have moved to the "Left". As the journalists have documented, those who are considered to be less advanced, have made "great strides".

These journalists are very thorough, as they have carefully made an investigation, in various states. In certain states, they expected a "Right Wing" candidate, someone who was a supporter of Trump, to be elected. Yet in many cases, this did not happen.

Those same journalists then conducted interviews, after the "midterms", within those certain states, in which they expected a Trump supporter to be elected. They have now concluded that "voters do not want extremists in office". They consider the "midterms" to be a "repudiation of Trumpism".

A happy thought!

I take a different view of the midterm elections. I regard it as an indication that the level of awareness of the common people, the working class, the proletariat, has just risen. Considerably, in fact.

As Lenin stated, quite clearly, in his excellent article, Left Wing Communism, An Infantile Disorder, "symptomatic of any genuine Revolution is a rapid, tenfold and even hundredfold increase in the size of the working and oppressed masses -hitherto apathetic- who are capable of waging the political struggle".

Without doubt, we are in the midst of a "genuine Revolution", as countless "working and oppressed" people, those who were "hitherto apathetic", are now becoming politically aware, prepared to take part in the "political struggle". Welcome, my Brothers and Sisters, my Comrades!

Now it is up to scientific socialists, by whom I of course mean Marxists, to bring to these people the awareness of the Revolutionary theories of Marx and Lenin.

The working class must be made aware of itself as a class, that of proletarians, with its own class interests. The proletarians have nothing to sell but their labour power. It is in their interests to sell themselves at the highest possible price. It is in the interests of the capitalists, the billionaires, the bourgeoisie, to pay their workers as little as possible. That which is in the best interests of one class, is in the worst interests of the other class. In scientific jargon, we say that the interests of the two classes is "diametrically opposed".

No one has ever accused the capitalists, the billionaires, of being "sweetly reasonable". Any worker who has ever asked for a raise can testify to that! On the contrary, they are strictly "one way". Their way! Whatever it takes to "make a buck"! Further, they are interested only in making ever more money! Those who have billions want more billions, and those who have hundreds of billions, want *Trillions!*

These billionaires, monopoly capitalists, are technically referred to as imperialists. They are completely devoid of any progressive characteristics. This is to say that they are reactionary. They are fully prepared to stoop to any depth, in order to maintain their wealth and power. They must be overthrown. That can only be done through Revolution.

Lenin goes into this quite well in another excellent work, Imperialism, the Highest Stage of Capitalism. That book too, I highly recommend.

The working class must also be made aware that it is not enough to simply overthrow the government. The existing state apparatus, which has been set up to crush and exploit the working class, must be *smashed!* Otherwise, the leaders of the Revolution will merely take over that state apparatus, and use it for their own purposes! In other words, they will set themselves up as the new rulers! Out of the frying pan, into the fire!

The existing state apparatus must be replaced with a new state apparatus, in the form of the Dictatorship of the Proletariat. This new state apparatus is absolutely necessary, as the capitalists will not resign themselves to their new lot in life! On the contrary, they will make every effort to restore their "paradise lost". They will plot and scheme endlessly! They must be crushed! Thoroughly! They must not be allowed to return to power, as they did in Russia and China!

Lenin went into this, in great detail, in another one his masterpieces, State and Revolution. That is especially relevant today!

We currently do not have any true Communist Party, by which I mean a Party which calls for the Dictatorship of the Proletariat. The touchstone of a true Communist!

But we do have the Internet! We also have a working class that is cultured, in the sense that most working people know how to read. With that in mind, may I suggest that all working people order, perhaps through the Internet, the articles by Lenin, I previously mentioned, as well as What Is To Be Done? An understanding of those articles will give workers a fine grounding in the basics of Marxism.

May I also suggest the Communist Manifesto, by Marx and Engels. They explain the growth and development of capitalism, as well as the ruin of all other classes, aside from the proletariat. They also mention one other detail, which is supremely relevant. At a time of Revolution, something interesting happens:

"entire sections of the ruling class are, by the advance of industry, precipitated into the proletariat, or are at least threatened in their conditions of existence. These also supply the proletariat with fresh elements of enlightenment and progress."

That is a rather accurate description of our current situation! Those who are current or former members of the "ruling class"', the bourgeoisie, are those who can "supply the proletariat with fresh elements of enlightenment and progress". In other words, bring to the proletariat -your new Comrades!- the awareness of the Revolutionary theories of Marx and Lenin. Feel free to put aside your feelings of bitterness and frustration -which is completely understandable!- and get on with your life. We are prepared to offer you a bright future!

I mean that sincerely! Think of us as your new friends, if only because that is precisely the case! True friends! Proletarian friends! Not bourgeois "friends", those who stab each other in the back! We will never betray you, our new friends!

Your services are urgently required. As almost all of the bourgeois go to university, no doubt you are aware of the Revolutionary theories of Marx and Lenin. Not that those theories are "taught" in university, as they are distorted. Even so, that makes the bourgeois aware of those theories.

Now is your chance to "make a difference", to "change the world". In the process, you can practically guarantee yourself a brighter future! Your past will not be held against you.

You can be involved in raising the level of awareness of the working class. Feel free to share your own experience, that of formerly working in the service of the capitalists, as an example. No doubt the reward for those years of service was nil!

Help to make working people aware of the Marxist Revolutionary theories, especially that of the Dictatorship of the Proletariat. Spread the message through social media. No doubt Councils, otherwise known as Soviets, have taken shape, as all Revolutions give rise to such organizations. Become involved with those Councils. Above all else, get together with other -former- middle class intellectuals, and take part in the formation of a true Communist Party, Dictatorship of the Proletariat. Discreetly, as otherwise the government agents will be sure to incarcerate you!

After the Revolution, those who are highly skilled, in various fields, will be paid accordingly. Professional people, such as doctors, nurses, engineers and managers, will be rewarded. The only difference is that under the Dictatorship of the Proletariat, there will be no back stabbing. We will make sure of that! People will work together! Teamwork! The atmosphere will be far more relaxed.

Yet first the capitalists have to be overthrown. In addition to that which I just mentioned, an Insurrection must be organized. Hopefully, it will be swift and accurate, as was the Russian October Revolution of 1917. That Insurrection was almost bloodless!

As I have covered that in a different article, there is no need to repeat it here.

There are more indications that the Revolution is gaining strength, here in North America. The press is reporting that the new Chief of Police, for the city of Ottawa, is making preparations for an "anticipated" second Freedom Convoy. The politicians are determined that the city of Ottawa will not be occupied again! We will see about that!

It is very likely that the government spy agencies have picked up some "chatter" on the Internet. The Truckers Protest has not been "killed". It was merely diverted, and then only temporarily.

It is significant that most Revolutions start with a strike in the transportation industry. From there they tend to spread, and spread quickly. At the moment, there are Revolutions that are raging in other countries. Soon, they will all "touch down" on the shores of North America. There is no time to waste.

As I write this, the news outlets just announced that the Democratic controlled House just passed the Omnibus Bill. No doubt, in two weeks, when the Republicans take control of the House, the "fur will fly". It is likely that nothing will be done in Washington. That could well be an improvement!

For the moment, it is clear that Revolutions, as well as "mass movements", which will lead to Revolutions, are raging around the world. Even the press admits that Iran is now experiencing a Revolution. It has spread to the neighbouring countries of Russia and China. Even the country of Afghanistan is now in turmoil, as women are protesting, burning their head scarfs and cutting their hair.

In the United Kingdom, the nurses are joining the paramedics, by going on strike. The postal workers and the railroad workers may soon join them. Further, it would appear that there is also a Revolution raging in Peru, as well as Chile. And this is just the beginning!

In the interests of raising the level of awareness of the working class, may I suggest singing the International, in locations and at times which most irritate the capitalists. Hopefully, this will attract the attention of the press, so that it will be broadcast on the evening news. If nothing else, be sure to record it and post it on social media.

Further, if there is one slogan that can best be used to raise the level of awareness of the working class, then that one slogan is the Dictatorship of the Proletariat. Lenin refers to this as the "touchstone" of a true Marxist! It is also the very slogan which the capitalists most hate. With good reason, I might add! All the more reason to make that term a household expression.

May I suggest that in all propaganda, all messages to Comrades on social media, all greetings, all posters and banners, that the slogan must be:

Dictatorship of the Proletariat!

www.ingramcontent.com/pod-product-compliance
Lightning Source LLC
Chambersburg PA
CBHW032058020426
42335CB00011B/404